THE SAVVY RESUME WRITER

Books & CD-ROMs by Drs. Ron and Caryl Krannich

101 Dynamite Answers to Interview Questions
101 Secrets of Highly Effective Speakers
201 Dynamite Job Search Letters
Best Jobs For the 21st Century
Change Your Job, Change Your Life
The Complete Guide to International Jobs and Careers
The Complete Guide to Public Employment
The Directory of Federal Jobs and Employers
Discover the Best Jobs for You!
Dynamite Cover Letters
Dynamite Networking For Dynamite Jobs
Dynamite Resumes
Dynamite Salary Negotiations
Dynamite Tele-Search
The Educator's Guide to Alternative Jobs and Careers
Find a Federal Job Fast!
From Air Force Blue to Corporate Gray
From Army Green to Corporate Gray
From Navy Blue to Corporate Gray
Get a Raise in 7 Days
High Impact Resumes and Letters
International Jobs Directory
Interview For Success
Job-Power Source CD-ROM
Jobs and Careers With Nonprofit Organizations
Jobs For People Who Love to Travel
Mayors and Managers
Moving Out of Education
Moving Out of Government
The Politics of Family Planning Policy
Re-Careering in Turbulent Times
Resumes & Job Search Letters For Transitioning Military Personnel
Savvy Interviewing
Savvy Resume Writer
Shopping the Exotic South Pacific
Treasures and Pleasures of Australia
Treasures and Pleasures of China
Treasures and Pleasures of Hong Kong
Treasures and Pleasures of India
Treasures and Pleasures of Indonesia
Treasures and Pleasures of Italy
Treasures and Pleasures of Paris and the French Riviera
Treasures and Pleasures of Singapore and Bali
Treasures and Pleasures of Thailand
Ultimate Job Source CD-ROM

The Savvy Resume Writer

The Behavioral Advantage

Ronald L. Krannich
Caryl Rae Krannich

IMPACT PUBLICATIONS
Manassas Park, Virginia

Library of Congress Cataloging-in-Publication Data

Krannich, Ronald L.
    The savvy resume writer : the behavioral advantage /
Ronald L. Krannich, Caryl Rae Krannich.
      p. cm.—(The career savvy series)
Includes bibliographical references and index.
ISBN 1-57023-124-9
      1. Resumes (Employment). I. Krannich, Caryl
Rae. II. Title. III. Series.
HF5383.K7216 1999
650.14—dc21   99-052711

Publisher: For information on Impact Publications, including current and forthcoming publications, authors, press kits, bookstore, and submission requirements, visit Impact's Web site: *www.impactpublications.com*

Publicity/Rights: For information on publicity, author interviews, and subsidiary rights, contact the Public Relations and Marketing Department: Tel. 703/361-7300 or Fax 703/335-9486.

Sales/Distribution: Bookstore sales are handled through Impact's trade distributor: National Book Network, 15200 NBN Way, Blue Ridge Summit, PA 17214, Tel. 1-800-462-6420. All other sales and distribution inquiries should be directed to the publisher: Sales Department, IMPACT PUBLICATIONS, 9104 Manassas Dr., Suite N, Manassas Park, VA 20111-5211, Tel. 703/361-7300, Fax 703/335-9486, or *careersavvy@impactpublications.com*

Book design by Kristina Ackley

Contents

PREFACE

Why write another resume book, you may ask. Because numerous changes are taking place in today's job market and workplace that require a different type of resume— a behavior-based resume that clearly communicates to employers that you are a "perfect fit" for the job. These resumes go far beyond the old chronological, functional, and combination distinctions as well as those resumes that stress skills, abilities, and accomplishments. Savvy resumes are behavior-based resumes that also lead to behavior-based interviews. They are all about *patterns of behavior* that largely determine one's success or failure at work.

Today's talent-driven economy has put increasing pressure on employers to make smart hiring decisions. The emphasis is on selecting the right people for the right job and ensuring they will be productive and happy with the company for many years to come. No longer can employers afford to hire fast and fire slow; savvy employers are learning to hire slow and fire fast.

The Savvy Resume Writer incorporates post-millennium thinking about individual and group behavior in the workplace. We argue for a different type of resume that truly reflects your *motivated patterns of behavior (MPB)*. It's this pattern—that goes beyond your specific knowledge, skills, and abilities (KSAs)—that employers want to know more about and, if appropriate, hire. The best way to help employers make the right hiring decision is to clearly communicate your motivated pattern of behavior in relation to their specific hiring needs. While savvy resumes include knowledge, skills, abilities, and accomplishments, as well as keywords for today's new electronic resumes, above all they stress how all of these elements come together in the form of a motivated pattern of behavior.

The pages that follow outline the key elements that go into producing a new behavior-based resume. They also outline the process for writing, producing, distributing, and following-up a savvy resume. While we include several illustrative examples, this is not an "example" book from which readers can creatively plagiarize in the process of creating their own unique resume. Our emphasis throughout this book is on developing the necessary skills for writing a savvy resume and continuing these skills into other job search phases, especially networking and interviewing. If you follow the principles outlined in the following chapters, you should be able to create a powerful behavior-based resume that will serve you well throughout your job search. You will conduct a very focused job search that clearly communicates to employers what you have done, can do, and will do for them in the future. Above all, your job search will become a very satisfying and rewarding career experience.

Whatever you do, make sure you know who you are in terms of your motivated pattern of behavior. Once you discover this pattern, you will be well on your way to a very exciting career which you helped uncover when you began writing a savvy resume.

THE SAVVY RESUME WRITER

1

Write a Savvy Resume

You've just heard about a great job opportunity. You discovered three interesting job listings on the Internet as well as two classified ads in the newspaper for someone with your qualifications. You want to put your resume online. A company asks you to fax a copy of your resume; another company wants it sent by email. You feel it's time to start looking for another job. You're planning to make a career change. You expect to attend a job fair next week. You received a call from someone who wants to talk to you about an opportunity with his firm. You plan to enter the job market soon. You need to see your boss about a raise.

All of these situations raise a familiar question: Do you have a resume that clearly communicates your qualifications to potential employers and other key people?

You Need a Savvy Resume

Whatever your situation, you need a resume to handle any of these situations. If you already have a resume, you probably need to update it, or at least re-evaluate it, according to the latest resume writing advice. If you don't have a resume, it's time you started building a savvy resume that commands the attention of those who can affect your future.

A *savvy resume* isn't the typical resume received by thousands of human resources departments each day. It's a behavior-based resume that follows key writing, production, distribution, and follow-up principles. It's an employer-oriented resume, because it speaks the language of employers who are looking for a new type of employee in today's highly competitive, talent-driven economy—energetic individuals who can clearly articulate desirable *patterns of behavior*. When you write a savvy resume, these patterns of behavior are revealed as a series of *accomplishments* related to your *motivated abilities and skills* (MAS).

Prepare For Today's New Job Market

The typical resume that gets distributed to thousands of employers each day is inappropriate for today's new job market. Rich in names and inclusive employment dates, these resumes tend to summarize work history—organized in reverse chronological order—which is embellished with listings of formal duties and responsibilities. Primarily focusing on the past, with little attention given to highlighting actual accomplishments or outcomes, these resumes say little or nothing about what the individual can do or will do in the future. They lack the capacity to predict future on-the-job performance. As such, these resumes are interesting historical documents as well as excellent references for writing obituaries. While employers may find these resumes interesting, in the end most are unenlightening documents: they give few clues for *predicting future performance*. After all, employers want to hire an individual's future—his ability to achieve predictable outcomes—not his past employment record.

Hiring and retention have become the hot-button issues in today's new economy. With unemployment at record lows and with talented employees difficult to recruit and retain, employers can no longer afford the luxury of making costly hiring mistakes. In fact, studies show that a hiring mistake, whether resulting in dismissal or resignation, costs an employer from 100 to 200 percent of the employee's salary as well as more in lost opportunity costs. Not surprisingly, in today's highly competitive economy, employers are paying more and more attention to specifying position requirements, screening candidates, and hiring individuals with the right sets of behaviors for their company. They are looking for the perfect "fit"—key competencies that individuals will bring to their organization.

The old days when job seekers focused on incorporating a lot of "dress for success" elements in their resumes (color and weight of paper) and interviews (the navy blue or gray suit) are fast disappearing as savvy employers look more and more at clearly defined sets of behaviors that go beyond superficial first impressions. Experience and qualifications are defined by specific sets of quantifiable behaviors. Employers are less interested in where you worked for X number of years than in what you specifically accomplished in terms of benefits for companies A, B, and C.

> ## Ask Yourself
>
> ☑ What makes me different from other candidates?
>
> ☑ Do I have what employers really want from me?
>
> ☑ What motivates me to do a good job?
>
> ☑ Does my resume clearly reflect what I do well and enjoy doing?
>
> ☑ Do I have a well-defined pattern of work behavior that is predictable?

A savvy resume is the logical extension of what more and more savvy employers are already doing—conducting behavior-based interviews. If you navigate today's job market with a savvy resume, as well as know how to handle behavior-based interviews, you should do very well in your job search. You'll rise above 90 percent of the other candidates who fail to respond to the basic needs of employers by primarily focusing on their work history.

Are You Savvy?

Just how well prepared are you for writing and distributing a savvy resume? If you already have a resume, take it out and evaluate it according to the following statements:

SCALE: 1 = strongly disagree   4 = agree
          2 = disagree   5 = strongly agree
          3 = maybe, not certain

1. My resume clearly states what I have done, can do, and will do for employers.   1 2 3 4 5

2. My resume includes an objective that reflects focused career goals.   1 2 3 4 5

3. My resume reflects a clear pattern of behavior that is readily identifiable to employers.   1 2 3 4 5

4. My resume summaries specific skills, abilities, and accomplishments that define my motivated pattern of behavior (MPB).   1 2 3 4 5

5. My resume reflects the fact that I have a clear understanding of who I am and what I want to do in the future.   1 2 3 4 5

6. I know which resume format works best for me.   1 2 3 4 5

7. My resume is designed to be scanned into a resume database.   1 2 3 4 5

8. I know how to properly transmit an email version of my resume. 1 2 3 4 5

9. I understand how keywords operate and have included a powerful "keyword summary" in my scannable resume. 1 2 3 4 5

10. I know when it's best to mail, fax, or email my resume. 1 2 3 4 5

11. I have a powerful cover letter that will accompany my resume. 1 2 3 4 5

12. I know which resume distribution methods work best. 1 2 3 4 5

13. I know how to network and conduct referral interviews with my resume. 1 2 3 4 5

14. I know how to use a resume at job fairs. 1 2 3 4 5

15. I can get headhunters to read my resume and include it in their database of potential candidates. 1 2 3 4 5

16. I can conduct an effective resume follow-up campaign that further advances my job search. 1 2 3 4 5

TOTAL

Now, add each number you circled to get an overall cumulative score. If your total is 70 or more, you are well on your way to writing and distributing a savvy resume that conforms to the principles and examples found in this book. This book should help you refine your savvy resume so you can eventually score a perfect 80 points. On the other hand, if you scored below 55 points, this book should help you develop a savvy resume designed for today's new job market. Indeed, you should re-take this quiz once you complete this book.

Renewed Importance of Resumes

Writing a resume should be more than a time-honored ritual or rite of passage for job seekers. It's a business of screening for certain types of behaviors or competencies appropriate for different types of workplaces. Indeed, within the past few years, the resume has taken on renewed importance because of the highly competitive and time-consuming nature of the job market. Employers increasingly focus on the *contents and language* of resumes to initially screen candidates. They expect to receive well-crafted resumes, as well as excellent cover letters, that reflect the best professional efforts of candidates. Since you are a stranger to most employers, your resume must be very special to make an excellent first impression on someone who may review hundreds of resumes each month. Most important of all, employers are increasingly looking for savvy resumes that identify clear patterns of behavior in the form of specific accomplishments, which, in turn, translate predictors of future performance. Only after they have had a chance to screen such a resume are they willing to invest time in interviewing a candidate.

One of the most important developments for resumes within the past five years has been the increasing role of the Internet in the job search. As more and more employers use the Internet for recruiting candidates, the resume has taken on renewed importance as the job seeker's most important calling card for conducting a relatively passive online job search. The structure and operation of Internet employment sites, as well as homepages of employers, is such that *the resume is the currency of the online job search*. Employers and headhunters alike search for qualified candidates by "keywords." If you understand how this medium operates, you will pay special attention to developing an electronic resume that is rich in keywords. Internet savvy job seekers frequently network online for information and transmit their resume by email.

Employers Have Specific Needs

If you want to write a resume that motivates employers to invite you to an interview, you must first understand the needs of employers. What they don't need is another typical historical resume from someone who thinks that qualifying for a job is all about a reverse chronological listing of education, skills, and experience. Employers have specific *performance needs* that go far beyond the standard resume language of education, skills, and experience.

> Since employers want to *hire your future,* they need to understand your past patterns of behavior in order to *predict your future performance.*

The needs of employers are very simple: they seek competent individuals who can come to their organization with a *pattern of accomplishments* that will result in improving the value of their operations. Since employers want to *hire your future*, they need to understand your past patterns of behavior in order to *predict your future performance*. Therefore, your resume must provide evidence, or **supports**, indicating you have a predictable pattern of performance that should result in accomplishing great things for the employer. In other words, in the eyes of the employer, you are a "perfect fit" for the job and the organization. If hired, you'll most likely continue doing well and enjoying your work with this employer.

Jobs Require Competencies

Understanding employer's needs also means focusing on their job requirements. Most jobs are designed in relation to other jobs. They involve clear **skill sets** for accomplishing goals. While most employers identify the skills required for a particular job in a position description, the job also may require many other skills, or **competencies**, that encompass both technical and interpersonal aspects of working in a particular organizational culture. Be sure you understand what those skill sets and competencies are when you write a resume and target it toward a specific employer.

Organizations Hire Patterns of Behaviors

The focus throughout this book is on how to best identify and communicate your **patterns of behavior** to employers. Yes, your behav-

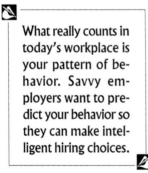

What really counts in today's workplace is your pattern of behavior. Savvy employers want to predict your behavior so they can make intelligent hiring choices.

ior—not just your education, skills, and work experience. What really counts in today's workplace is your pattern of behavior. Savvy employers increasingly want to predict your behavior so they can make intelligent hiring choices. Without an understanding of your behavior, an employer is likely to make another hiring mistake, especially when they discover you have a pattern of behavior that is not conducive to their organizational values. If you can help an employer better understand your pattern of behavior as being directly related to their needs, you will be in a very strong position to be "screened in" for a job interview. You begin doing this by incorporating a series of relevant accomplishments in your savvy resume and letter.

Acquire the Behavioral Advantage

Make sure you navigate today's job market with a savvy resume that gives you the behavioral advantage. You have the behavioral advantage when your resume clearly communicates that you are the perfect "fit" for a position. Not only do you want to convince employers that you are the right candidate for the job, you also want to make sure the job best "fits" you: it should be directly related to your motivated abilities and skills (MAS)—those things you do well and enjoy doing on a regular and recurring basis (your behavioral pattern). Employers increasingly want to hire individuals who can communicate their "qualifications" in such behavioral terms.

2

RESUME ISSUES AND RULES

Resume writing is often viewed as a rite of passage or a necessary evil—something you must do, often grudgingly, in order to get a job. It's not something most people look forward to doing with enthusiasm. After all, it's a very ego-involved, rejection-ridden activity. You have to summarize, in the space of one or two pages, who you are in terms of your work and professional capabilities. You must tell strangers what you have done in the past so they will be interested enough to call you for an interview.

The Reluctant Resume Writer

Not surprisingly, most people are reluctant resume writers. They write a resume because that's what they are expected to do if they want to play the job search game. They basically are motivated by fear and possible negative consequences. Indeed, without a resume, strangers will not know who you are and what you can do. So you need a resume.

But what kind of resume should you write? Will it include an objective? How long should it be? Do you need more than one version of your resume? What's the proper way to present your work experience and education? Should you include personal information and references on your resume?

10

Better still, what exactly are employers looking for on resumes these days? What kind of resume language works best in today's job market? How many "keywords" should you include on your resume? What are the chances your resume will be scanned into a resume database? If you email your resume, will it look good to the reader? When should you fax or email your resume to an employer?

Reluctant resume writers often lack good answers to these questions. But savvy resume writers know exactly what needs to be done in order to produce and distribute a powerful resume that gets job interviews. They approach their task with solid information on what works and doesn't work with today's employers. They also approach the resume writing task with enthusiasm. After all, their new resume will be an important ticket to renewed career success. If done properly, their new resume can mean a significant increase in income and an enhanced career because it opened the right doors to renewed career success.

If you are a reluctant resume writer, let's make sure you become a savvy resume writer by approaching this subject with enthusiasm, determination, and dogged persistence. In today's new talent-driven economy, you need to present your very best self to potential employers—that part of you that assures employees that you are the best "fit" for the job and that they made a wise hiring choice.

What Resumes Used to Be

Resumes are many different things to many different people. Unfortunately, most people still have a very traditional view of a resume. This view prevents them from creating an effective resume. In fact, not knowing the secrets of savvy resume writers, they continue to make many resume writing and distribution mistakes that lead to numerous rejections.

The hardest part of advising people on how to write an effective resume is in convincing them that they need to start over with an all-new resume. They need to be open to a new approach which usually means scrapping their much loved resume. The problem is often this: many people already have a resume they really like. After all, they read it numerous times, and liked it more each time. They even showed it off to their friends and relatives who also said they liked it. Not knowing any better and saddled with their ego, they resist new ideas or only incorporate a few new ideas into revising what is essentially an ineffective resume for a bygone era.

What exactly is a resume? According to most people, it's a summary of one's work history. In other words, it's your work obituary. If you define a resume in this matter, chances are you will create a resume that indeed looks like an obituary—it lists in reverse chronological order each job you held and then summarizes the duties and responsibilities for each job. In the end, this "chronological resume" tells employers that you have so many years of work experience performing X, Y, and Z jobs. Emphasizing names, inclusive employment dates, job titles, and duties and responsibilities, such resumes tell employers little or nothing about what you actually *accomplished*. Did you, for example, save the company $200,000 by developing an innovative program for cutting production costs? Did your efforts in redesigning your sales team result in $500,000 in increased sales for each team member? Did your improved customer service program increase the number of repeat sales

Ask Yourself

☑ What do employers look for on resumes?

☑ Does my resume include a career objective?

☑ Should I include personal statements?

☑ How will I distribute my resume and to whom?

☑ Have I outlined my key accomplishments?

☑ What's the best way to follow-up a resume?

by 20 percent? Does your resume communicate that you have a consistent pattern of developing innovative solutions to scheduling problems that result in the improved operations of a company? Exactly what pattern of behavior will an employer expect to hire based on reading your chronological resumes.

Chances are your chronological resume provides few if any clues to answering such behavior-based questions that relate to results. In fact, these resumes are structurally incapable of providing answers or clues to these questions because the whole resume is poorly defined and conceived. Let's redefine your resume. Instead of being a summary of your work history, why not view a resume as a statement of qualifications an employer seeks. In other words, your resume tells an employer whether or not you have the right pattern of behavior to perform the job in question. It tells the employer three very important things:

1. Here is what I have accomplished in the past.

2. Here is what I am likely to accomplish for you in the future.

3. Let's talk about how my core competencies will benefit your operations.

This is a savvy resume, one designed for today's savvy employer who looks for individuals who are the "right fit" for the job. This is the type of resume you should be writing for strengthening your future employability.

Major Myths and Realities

Over the years we have encountered numerous resume myths that prevent individuals from being effective in their job search. Many of these myths relate to the basic definition of a resume. Other myths indicate a basic lack of understanding of how the job market operates and what employers are really looking for in today's job market. These myths affect each resume stage, from writing to production, distribution, and follow-up. Among the most important resume myths are these:

Job Finding Myths

MYTH 1: **The best way to find a job is to respond to classified ads, use employment agencies, submit applications, get your resume into online databases, respond to Internet job listings, and mail resumes and cover letters to human resources offices.**

REALITY: Many people do get jobs by following such formalized application and recruitment procedures. This is basically a queue approach to finding a job: candidates put themselves in the queue in the hope that their resume or application will move to the front. However, these are not necessarily the best ways to get the best jobs—those offering good pay, advancement opportunities, and an appropriate "fit" with one's skills, abilities, and goals. The best way to get a job is to target specific employers who are in need of your competencies. You do this by networking for information, advice, and referrals. Your resume plays a key role in the process.

Classified ads, agencies, and personnel offices tend to list low paying yet highly competitive jobs. Most of the best jobs—high level, excellent pay, least competitive—are neither listed nor advertised; they are uncovered through word-of-mouth. When seeking employment, your most fruitful strategy will be to conduct research and informational interviews on what is called the "hidden job market."

MYTH 2: **A good resume and cover letter will get me a job.**

REALITY: There's nothing magical about a resume or letter. In fact, many people confuse the role of resumes and letters in a job search. Resumes and letters do not get jobs—they at best advertise you for interviews. Your resume and letters are **marketing tools** designed to communicate your qualifications to employers. From the perspective of employers, resumes and letters are used to screen candidates—who are basically strangers to employers—for interviews. Few people ever get hired on the basis of their resume and letters. When surveyed, over 95% of employers indicate they hire on the basis of a personal interview. If you believe your cleverly crafted resume and letters have some magical quality, you may end up engaging in a whole series of useless—and embarrassing—resume and letter writing activities. Knowing this, you should write your resume and letters with the idea of persuading readers to call you for an interview. Your writing skills must move the reader to take such action.

MYTH 3: **The candidate with the best education, skills, and experience usually gets the job.**

REALITY: Employers hire individuals for many different reasons. In the end, they either benefit or suffer from their employees' *patterns of behavior* which affect the quality of the organization. After working with someone for several months, most employers know how to "read" or stereotype an employee in terms of his or her behavioral patterns. Some employees, for example, are always responsible and dependable. Others take a great deal of initiative, energize co-workers, consistently come up with good ideas, and follow-through with results. And still others exhibit marginal behavior; they need to be closely supervised, expand their work to the time available, make the same recurring excuses, avoid responsibilities, and lack common sense and initiative. In other words, most employee behavior becomes both *patterned and predictable* after a while. Savvy employers understand this and thus would like to know what your particular pattern of behavior is *before* putting you on the payroll and then learning about your particular pattern six months down the road—when it may be time to fire you because you are a poor "fit" (you have an inappropriate pattern of behavior) for the organization.

> Most employee behavior becomes both *patterned and predictable* after a while. Savvy employers would like to know what your particular pattern of behavior is *before putting you on the payroll*...

Education, skills, and experience—standard information categories appearing on most resumes—tell employers nothing about your behavioral patterns. These are basically a few of several *screening criteria* for selecting candidates for a job interview. Surprising to some candidates, these criteria may **not** be the most important *hiring criteria* in the eyes of employers. If, for example, employers only hired on the basis of education, skills, and experience, they would not need to interview candidates. Such static and redundant information is available in applications and on resumes. Employers interview because they are looking for *other competencies* that are best assessed in face-to-face interviews. They want to see a warm body—how you look and interact with them and how you might fit into their organization. They are concerned about your communication and social skills and whether or not you are appropriate for the culture of their organization. They can get all the other "qualifications" information from additional sources. Indeed, the most important reason for hiring you is that the employer "likes" you. How "likes" is defined will vary from one employer and organization to another. In some cases the employer "likes" you because of your educational background, demonstrated skills, and experience. In other cases the employer "likes" you because of your style and personality as well as a gut feeling that you are the right person for the job. He or she may even like you because of your age, gender, ethnicity, memberships, or old school ties. The employer will determine or confirm these feelings in the actual job interview. So be prepared in the job interview to communicate a great deal of information about yourself other than what the employer already knows from your resume—education, skills, and experience. Focus on your pattern of behavior in the form of specific and recurring types of accomplishments. Be prepared to answer behavior-based questions, such as:

Tell me about when you saved Company Y . . .

What would you do if . . .

What accomplishments have you been especially proud of during the past 3 years?

What does your current employer see as your 3 major contributions to his operations?

Tell me about a recent time you took responsibility for something that was outside of your job description.

Also, be prepared to *ask questions* that indicate you have the right motivation and competencies to do the job. Most important of all, make yourself memorable to *everyone* you meet at the interview. And remember, this whole process starts with your savvy resume!

MYTH 4: **You can plan all you want, but getting a job is really a function of good luck.**

REALITY: Luck is a function of being in the right place at the right time to take advantage of opportunities that come your way. But how do you plan your luck? The best way to have luck come your way is to plan to be in many different places at many different times. You can do this by putting together an excellent resume and marketing it within both the advertised and hidden job markets. If you are redundant, persistent, and tenacious—rather than aggressive, obnoxious, and pushy—in implementing your plans, luck may strike you many times!

Resume Content and Writing Myths

MYTH 5: **The best type of resume is one that outlines employment history by job titles, responsibilities, and inclusive employment dates.**

REALITY: Ugh! This is a prescription for job search failure or for hiring a potential "misfit." Avoid this type of traditional chronological or "obituary" resume. It's filled with historical "what" information—what work you did, in what organizations, over what period of time. It tells employers little about what it is you can do for them. You should choose a resume format that clearly communicates your major strengths—not your history—to employers in relation to your goals and skills as well as the employer's needs. Your best choice will be the combination or hybrid resume.

MYTH 6: **It's unnecessary to put an objective on the resume.**

REALITY: What ties your resume together in communicating to employers what it is you both want and can do? An objective—stated at the very top of your resume; it becomes the central focus from which all other elements in your resume should flow. The objective gives the resume organization and coherence. It tells employers exactly who you are in terms of your goals and skills. If properly stated, your objective will become the most powerful and effective statement on your resume. Without an objective, you force the employer to "interpret" your resume. He or she must analyze and synthesize the discreet elements in each of your categories and draw conclusions about your capabilities and goals which may or may not be valid. Therefore, it is to your advantage to set the agenda—control the flow and interpretation of your qualifications and capabilities by stating the objective. Most people who object to including an objective on a resume (1) do not understand the importance of integrating all elements in the resume around key goals and skills, (2) do not know how to develop a good employer-centered objective, or (3) are misinformed because they believe they must change the objective for each employer—an obvious confession they do not know what they really want to do. Developing a resume objective is not a difficult task. If nothing else, stating an objective on your resume is a thoughtful thing to do for the employer. And always remember, employers "like" thoughtful people!

> The objective gives the resume organization and coherence. If properly stated, it will become the most powerful and effective statement on your resume.

MYTH 7: **Most employers appreciate long resumes because they present more complete information for screening candidates than short resumes.**

REALITY: Employers prefer receiving one- or two-page resumes. Longer resumes lose the interest and attention of readers. They usually lack a focus, are filled with extraneous information, need editing, and are oriented toward the applicant's past rather than the employer's future. If you know how to write a savvy resume, you can put all of your competencies into a one- to two-page format. These resumes only include enough information to persuade employers to call you for an interview. But this one- to two-page rule does not apply to all employment situations. Individuals applying for academic and international jobs, for example, may be expected to write a five- to ten-page curriculum vita (CV) rather than a one- to two-page resume. In these special situations the CV is actually a traditional chronological resume prominently displaying dates, job titles, responsibilities, and publications.

MYTH 8:   **It's okay to put salary expectations on a resume.**

REALITY: Never, never, never. One of the worst things you can do is to mention salary on your resume. Remember, the purpose of your resume is to get an interview. Only during the interview—and preferably toward the very end—should you discuss salary. But before you discuss salary, you want to demonstrate your **value** to employers as well as learn about the **worth** of the position. Only after you make your impression and gather information on the job, can you realistically talk about—and negotiate—salary. You can not do this if you prematurely mention salary on your resume.

MYTH 9:   **Contact information (name, address, phone number, email) should appear in the left-hand corner of your resume.**

REALITY: You can choose from a variety of resume formats which place the contact information in several different positions at the top of the resume. Choose the one that best complements the remaining layout and style of the resume.

MYTH 10: **You should not include your hobbies or any personal statements on a resume.**

REALITY: In general this is true. However, there are exceptions which would challenge this rule as a myth. If you have a hobby or a personal statement that can strengthen your objective in relation to the employer's needs, do include it on your resume. For example, if a job calls for someone who is outgoing and energetic, you would not want to include a hobby or personal statement that indicates that you are a very private and sedentary person, such *"Enjoy reading and writing"* or *"Collect stamps."* But *"Enjoy organizing community fund drives"* and *"Compete in the Boston Marathon"* might be very appropriate statements for your resume. Such statements further emphasize the "unique you" in relation to your capabilities, the requirements for the position, and the employer's needs. Remember, one of your goals is to get the employer to "like" you. If carefully selected, some hobbies and personal statements can provide important personal linkages to the employer.

MYTH 11: **You should list your references on the resume so the employer can check them before conducting the interview.**

REALITY: Never include references on your resume. The closest you should ever get to doing so is to include this statement at the very end: *"References available upon request."* **You** want to control your references for the interview. You should take a list of references appropriate for the position you will interview for with you to the interview. The interviewer may ask you for this list at the end of the interview. If you put references on your resume, the employer might call someone who has no idea you are applying for a particular job. The conversation could be embarrassing. As a simple courtesy, you should ask the person's permission to use them as a reference. This will alert them that someone may call and gives you the opportunity to brief them about the position and how your skills fit the employer's needs. Focus on your goals and strengths in relation to the position. Surprisingly, many employers don't follow-through by contacting references.

Resume Production Myths

MYTH 12:   **You should try to get as much as possible on each page of your resume.**

REALITY: Each page of your resume should be appealing to the eye. It should make an immediate favorable impression, be inviting and easy to read, and look professional. You achieve these qualities by using a variety of layout, type style, highlighting, and emphasizing techniques. When formatting each section of your resume, be sure to make generous use of white space. Bullet and underline items for emphasis. If you try to cram a great deal on each page, your resume will look cluttered and uninviting to the reader. However, make sure you do not over-use such emphasizing techniques.

MYTH 13: **You should have your resume typeset and professionally printed.**

REALITY: It's not necessary to go to the expense of typesetting
and printing given today's computer technology with
powerful word processing and desktop publishing programs. Most word processors, using letter-quality printers, produce good quality type, and many copy machines will give you near original quality copies. If
you use a word processor, make sure you use a letter
quality or laser printer. Dot matrix printers and many
near letter quality printers do not produce professional
copy. They look mass produced.

MYTH 14: **The weight and color of the resume's paper and
ink is unimportant to employers.**

REALITY: Weight, paper color, and ink do count if you are sending your resume by mail to a specific person. If you
are faxing or emailing your resume, this becomes a
non-issue. Paper color and quality are the very first
things the employer sees and feels when receiving your
resume by mail. They make an important initial impression. If your resume doesn't look and feel right
during the first five seconds, the reader may not feel
good about reading the contents of your resume. Make
a good initial impression by selecting a good weight
and color of paper. Your resume should have a sub-
stantive feel to the touch—use nothing less than
20-pound paper which also has some texture. But
don't go to extremes with a very heavy and roughly
textured paper. Stay with conservative paper colors:

white, off- white, ivory, light tan, or light grey. Your choice of ink colors should also be conservative— black, navy, or dark brown. If, on the other hand, you are applying for a less conventional position, especially one in graphic design, fine arts, film, interior design, or advertising, where creativity is encouraged on resumes, you may decide to go with more daring paper and ink colors. We still like resumes printed on good quality white paper with black ink.

MYTH 15: **You should make at least 100 copies of your resume.**

REALITY: Make only as many as you need—which may be only one. Since it's not necessary to have your resume professionally printed and since many copy machines produce excellent quality copies, you have the flexibility to produce as many as you need. If you produce your resume on a word processor, you can customize each resume for each position for which you apply. Your production needs should be largely determined by your strategy for distributing your resume.

Letter Writing Myths

MYTH 16: **It's okay to send your resume to an employer without an accompanying cover letter.**

REALITY: Only if you want the employer to think his or her position and employment opportunity are not important. This myth is propagated by those who believe employers are too busy to read but not too busy to be pestered by cold telephone calls and networkers who invite themselves to interviews. Employers initially prefer succinct written communications. It enables them to screen candidates in and out for the next stage of the hiring process—a telephone screening interview. Sending a resume without a cover letter is like going to a job interview barefoot—your application is incomplete and your resume is not being properly communicated for action. Cover letters should always accompany resumes that are sent through the mail. They help position your interests and qualifications in relation to the employer's needs as well as indicate what action will be taken next. Above all, they give employers signals of your personality, style, and likability—important elements in the hiring decision.

> Cover letters help position your interests and qualifications in relation to the employer's needs. They give employers signals of your personality, style, and likability.

MYTH 17: **The purpose of a cover letter is to introduce your resume to an employer.**

REALITY: A cover letter should be much more than mere cover for a resume. Indeed, it may be a misnomer to call these letters "cover letters." It's best to think of them as "interview generating" communications—a form of written communication that goes beyond the resume. Unlike a resume which tends to follow a standard, conventional format, in a cover letter you can be more creative and unconventional. If written properly, the cover letter format enables you to express important qualities sought by employers in the job interview—your personality, style, energy, and enthusiasm. Like good advertising copy, your cover letter should be the "sizzle" or headline accompanying your savvy resume. After all, the purpose of a cover letter should be to get the employer to **take action** on your resume. Consequently, the whole structure of your cover letter should focus on persuading the employer to invite you for a job interview. Make your cover letter grab the attention of the reader who will be interested enough to read your resume in depth and call you for an interview.

MYTH 18: End your letter indicating that you expect to hear from the employer: *"I look forward to hearing from you."*

REALITY: What do you expect will happen when you close your letter in this manner? Probably nothing. While this is a polite and acceptable way of closing such a letter, it is a rather empty statement of hope—not one of action. Remember, you always want specific **actions** to result from your written communication. Any type of action—positive or negative—should help you move on to the next stage of your job search with this or other potential employers. This standard closing is likely to result in no action on the part of the employer who is by definition a busy person. It's better to indicate that **you** will take initiative in contacting the employer in response to your letter and resume. End your letter with an action statement like this one:

> *I'll give you a call Thursday afternoon to answer any questions you may have regarding my interests and qualifications.* Be there,

Such an action statement, in effect, invites you to a telephone interview—the first step to getting a face-to-face job interview. While some employers may avoid your telephone call, at least you will get some action in reference to your letter and resume. If, for example, you call on Thursday afternoon and the employer is not available to take your call, leave a message that you called in reference to your letter. Chances are the employer is expecting your call and will remember you because you are taking this initiative. In some cases, the employer will tell you frankly that you are no longer under consideration. While disappointing, this rejection has a positive side—it clarifies your status so you no longer need to waste your time nor engage in wishful thinking about the status of your application with this employer. Go on to others who may prove more responsive. In other cases, your phone call may result in getting a face-to-face interview early in the application process with this employer. Taking action in this manner will at least give you useful information that will bring your application nearer to closure. But make sure you call at the time you say you will call. If the employer expects your call on Thursday afternoon and you forget to do so, you prematurely communicate a negative message to the employer—you lack follow-through. Always do what you say you will do and in a timely fashion.

MYTH 19: **The cover letter should attempt to sell the employer on your qualifications.**

REALITY: The cover letter should command attention and nicely provide a cover for an enclosure—your resume. This letter should be professional, polite, personable, and to the point. The letter affords you an opportunity to demonstrate your personality and writing skills in a letter format. Remember, your resume is supposed to sell the employer on you. Your letter should be the sizzle accompanying the sale. The letter should mention your interest in the position, highlight your major strengths in relation to the position, and ask the employer for an opportunity to interview for the position. Avoid repeating in this letter what the reader will find in your resume. Keep the letter to one page.

> **Your resume is supposed to sell the employer on you. Your letter should be the sizzle accompanying the sale.**

MYTH 20:   **Handwritten cover letters have a greater impact on employers than typewritten cover letters.**

REALITY: Handwritten cover letters are inappropriate as are scribbled notes on or attached to a resume. They are **too** personal and look unprofessional when applying for a job. If you are a professional, you want to demonstrate that you can present yourself to others in the most professional manner possible. Confine your handwriting activities to your signature only. The letter should be typed on a good quality machine—preferably a letter quality printer. If you use a word processor, it's best to justify the left margin only.

MYTH 21: **Letters are not very important in a job search. The only letter you need to write is a formal cover letter.**

REALITY: Your letters actually may be more important than your resume. In fact, cover letters are only one of several types of letters you should write during your job search. The other letters are some of the best kept secrets of effective job seekers. They may become your most powerful marketing tools:

- Resume letters
- Approach letters
- Thank-you letters

Different types of thank-you letters should be written on various job search occasions:

- Post-job interview
- After informational interview
- Responding to a rejection
- Withdrawing from consideration
- Accepting job offer
- Terminating employment

Each of these letters can be structured in a variety of ways. The powerful letters tend to be structured as "T" Letters. For example, see *Haldane's Best Cover Letters for Professionals* (Impact, 2000).

These are some of the most neglected yet most important forms of written communications in any job search. If you write these letters, your job search may take you much further than you expected!

Distribution Myths

MYTH 22: **It is best to send out numerous resumes and letters to prospective employers in the hope that a few will invite you to an interview.**

REALITY: Yes, if you play the odds, someone might call you. If you broadcast your resume to 1,000 employers, you may receive two or three interviews. However, this broadcast approach is most appropriate for people who are in desperate need of a job or who don't know what they want to do. They tend to communicate a "give-me-a-job" mentality. Such a non-focused approach will initially give you a false sense of making progress with your job search because it involves a major expenditure of time and money. But it will most likely increase your level of frustration when you receive few replies, with most of those being rejections. You should avoid this approach. Instead, concentrate on targeting your resume on particular organizations, employers, and positions that would best fit into your particular mix of skills and objectives. This approach requires networking for information and job leads. In so doing, you will seldom send a resume and cover letter through the mail. Instead, you will write numerous approach and thank-you letters for the purpose of inviting yourself to interviews. Your resume should never accompany these letters.

MYTH 23: **When conducting an informational interview, you should present your resume at the beginning of the meeting.**

REALITY: Never ever introduce yourself with your resume. Instead, your resume should be presented at the very **end** of the informational interview. Keep in mind that the purpose of an informational interview is to get information, advice, and referrals. You are not asking for a job. If you present your resume at the beginning of such an interview, you give the impression that you are looking for a job. Near the end of the interview you want to ask the interviewer to review your resume and give you advice on how to strengthen it and to whom to send it.

Follow-Up Myths

MYTH 24: **Once you distribute your resume and letters, there is little you can do other than wait to be called for an interview.**

REALITY: If you do nothing, you are likely to get nothing. There are many things you can do. First, you can write more letters to inquire about your application status. Second, you can telephone the employer for more information on when the interview and hiring decisions will take place. Third, you can telephone to request an interview at a convenient time. The first approach will likely result in no response. The second approach will probably give you an inconclusive answer. The third approach will give you a *"yes"* or *"no."* We prefer the third approach.

MYTH 25: **The best way to follow-up on your application and resume is to write a letter of inquiry.**

REALITY: Employers are busy people who do not have time to read all their mail, much less sit down to write letters. Use the telephone instead. It's much more efficient and effective. Most important of all, you should monitor your resumes and letters by keeping records and regularly follow up on your job search initiatives. Be sure to keep good records of all correspondence, telephone conversations, and meetings. Keep a separate paper or electronic file on each prospective employer. Record your contact information and dates for all employers on a master record form so you can quickly evaluate the present status of your contacts as well as use it as a handy reference.

Electronic and Multimedia Resume Myths

MYTH 26: **Electronic resumes are the wave of the future. You must write and distribute them in order to get a good job.**

REALITY: Electronic resumes (scannable, emailable, HTML, video, and multimedia) are increasingly important for job seekers and employers alike. More and more employers use the latest resume scanning technology to quickly screen hundreds of resumes or request that resumes be transmitted over the Internet via email. Therefore, it also may be in your interest to write "computer friendly" and email versions of your resume based on the principles of electronic resumes. These principles, along with examples, are outlined in several resume books: Peter Weddle, *Internet Resumes* (Impact, 1998); Pat Criscito, *Resumes in Cyberspace*

(Barrons, 1997); and Fred Jandt and Mary Nemnich, *Cyberspace Resume Kit* (JIST, 1999). Electronic resumes are very different resumes compared to conventional resumes. The scannable versions are structured around "keywords" or nouns which stress capabilities. While such resumes may be excellent candidates for resume scanners and electronic employment databases, they may be weak documents for human readers. Keep in mind that scannable resumes are primarily written for electronic scanners and high-tech distribution systems (employment databases) rather than for human beings. Since human beings interview and hire, you should first create a savvy resume that follows the principles of human communication. We also recommend developing separate resumes designed for electronic scanners and email transmission. We're less enthusiastic about HTML, video, and multimedia resumes because they incorporate too many elements that should be left to the actual fact-to-face job interview.

MYTH 27: **Individuals who include their resumes in resume banks or post them online in resume databases are more likely to get high paying jobs than those that don't.**

REALITY: During the past five years most electronic resume banks have become victims of the "free" Internet. Most have either gone out of business or have transformed their operations by becoming resume databases on the Internet. While some resume banks and databases still charge users monthly or yearly membership fees, most are now supported by employers who advertise on the sites and/or pay fees to access resumes online through particular Internet employment sites. Essentially a high-tech approach for broadcasting resumes, inclusion of your resume in these resume banks and databases means your resume literally works 24-hours a day. Major employers increasingly use these resume banks and databases for locating qualified candidates, especially for screening individuals with technical skills. And we know some individuals who join these resume banks do get jobs. However, there is no evidence that most people belonging to these groups get interviews or jobs through such membership. Nor is there evidence that membership results in higher paying jobs than nonmembership. The real advantage of such groups is this:

> Membership groups open new channels for contacting employers whom you might not otherwise come into contact with. Employers also turn to the Internet as a cheaper method for recruiting.

they open new channels for contacting employers whom you might not otherwise come into contact with. Indeed, some employers only use these resume banks and databases for locating certain types of candidates rather than use more traditional channels, such as newspapers and employment offices, for advertising positions and recruiting candidates. Employers find the Internet to be a much cheaper way of recruiting personnel than through the more traditional approach of purchasing classified ads or hiring employment firms or headhunters. For the employer's perspective on using the Internet for recruitment purposes, see Ray Schreyer and John McCarter, *The Employer's Guide to Recruiting Jobs On the Internet* (Manassas Park, VA: Impact Publications, 1998).

MYTH 28: **The video resume is the wave of the future. You need to develop a video resume and send it to prospective employers.**

REALITY: The video resume is a novel approach to the employment process. However, since it is video-based, it's really a misnomer to call these videos a form of "resume." The so-called video resume functions more as a screening interview than a resume. Remember, the purpose of a resume is to get an interview. A video includes key elements that are best presented in a face-to-face interview—verbal and nonverbal communication. Unless requested by an employer in lieu of a traditional resume, we recommend avoiding the use of the video resume. However, if you are applying for a position that requires good presentation skills best demonstrated in the video format, such as in sales, broadcasting, and entertainment, the video resume may be useful. But make sure you do a first-class job in developing the video. Avoid amateur products which will probably reflect badly on your skills.

MYTH 29: **You should develop your own homepage on the Internet and direct employers to your site.**

REALITY: Do this only if you are a real professional and can customize your site to particular employers. Like the video resume, homepages can be double-edged swords. Some employers may like them, but others may dislike them. Your particular site may reflect poorly on your qualifications, especially if it is not designed like a resume, i.e., stresses your accomplishments and goals. Furthermore, since most employers are too busy trying to get through paper resumes and letters, few have the time or desire to spend time accessing your Internet site—unless your paper resume and letter sufficiently motivate them to do so. Like viewing videos, accessing sites on the Internet takes time. Remember, employers can still screen a paper resume and letter within 30 seconds! Why would they want to spend 15 minutes trying to access and review your site when they could be dispensing with another 30 resumes and letters during that time? If you decide to go this route, you'll need to give employers a good reason why they should invest such time looking for you on the Internet!

But these myths and realities only touch the surface of understanding how to create savvy resumes and letters. You also need to know something about common resume errors. Employers report observing numerous resume errors, from writing to follow-up, that candidates should avoid.

Mistakes You Shouldn't Make

A savvy resume follows certain rules that increase the possibility it will get read. Most of these rules relate to a series of deadly resume errors reported by employers. The most common mistakes occur when writers fail to keep the purpose of their resume in mind.

> Every time you make an error, you provide supports for eliminating you from further consideration. Concentrate, instead, on providing supports for being considered for a job interview.

Most errors kill a resume even before it gets fully read—the resume is literally "dead upon arrival." At best these errors leave negative impressions which are difficult to overcome at this or any other point in the hiring process. Remember, hiring officials have two major inclusion/exclusion concerns in mind when reading your resume:

- They are looking for excuses to eliminate you from further consideration.

- They are looking for evidence to consider you for a job interview—how much value you will add to their operations.

Every time you make an error, you provide *supports* for eliminating you from further consideration. Concentrate, instead, on providing supports for being considered for a job interview.

Make sure your resume is not "dead on arrival." To ensure against this, avoid these most 20 common writing errors reported by employers:

20 Common Resume Writing Errors

1. Not related to the employer's interests or needs; experience irrelevant to the position under consideration.

2. Too long, short, or condensed.

3. Poorly designed format and an unattractive appearance.

4. Misspellings, bad grammar, and wordiness.

5. Poor punctuation.

6. Lengthy phrases, sentences, and paragraphs.

7. Too slick, amateurish, or "gimmicky."

8. Too boastful or dishonest.

9. Critical categories, experience, and skills missing.

10. Poorly organized—hard to understand or requires too much interpretation.

11. Unexplained time gaps.

12. Does not convey accomplishments or a pattern of performance from which the reader can predict future performance.

13. Text does not support objective.

14. Unclear or vague objective.

15. Lacks credibility and content—includes lots of fluff and "canned" resume language.

16. Appears over-qualified or under-qualified for the position.

17. Includes a photo and lots of personal information, such as height, weight, and age.

18. Lacks sufficient contact information (i.e., telephone or fax number) or appears somewhat anonymous (uses a P.O. Box for an address).

19. Constantly refers to "I" and appears self-centered—fails to clearly communicate what he or she will likely do for the employer.

20. Includes "red flag" information such as being fired or incarcerated, confessing health or performance problems, or stating salary figures, including salary requirements that may be too high or too low.

This listing of writing errors and possible reader responses emphasizes how important *both* form and content are when writing a resume with purpose. You must select an appropriate form, arrange each element in an attractive manner, and provide the necessary substance to grab the attention of the reader and move him or her to action. And all these elements of good resume writing must be related to the needs of your audience. If not, you may quickly kill your resume by committing some of these deadly errors.

Remember, hiring officials are busy people who only devote a few seconds to reading a resume. They quickly identify errors that will effectively remove you from consideration. They want to see you error-free on paper so they can concentrate on what they most need to do—evaluate your qualifications.

While writing errors are the most common reasons for eliminating candidates from consideration, several other errors relate to the production, distribution, and follow-up of resumes. We'll examine several of these additional errors, as well as rules for success, when we examine key resume production, distribution, and follow-up issues in Chapters 6-9.

3

THE NEW BEHAVIORAL RESUME

In some respects, our behavioral resume is nothing new. What is new is how this type of resume presents your competencies *as a whole* around a well-targeted objective. It goes far beyond mere experience, skills, abilities, and accomplishments, which are often seen as the defining elements in one's "qualifications."

Go Beyond Accomplishments

For years, many career experts have emphasized how important it is to communicate your *accomplishments* to employers during the job search. They've stressed the importance of doing first things first—assess your skills and abilities and develop a well-targeted job/career objective *before* writing and distributing your resume to potential employers. By focusing on your accomplishments, you clearly let employers know what it is you have done in the past, can do at present, and will do for them in the future. Your accomplishments are the basic building blocks for understanding and predicting your overall work performance. They are the basic elements that appear on annual performance appraisals and help determine raises and promotions. Strangely, though, accomplishments are often absent on resumes and are not probed in much depth during job interviews, unless the employer conducts behavior-based interviews.

It's the Motivated Pattern That Really Counts

But focusing on accomplishments alone is not what's most important in conducting a successful job search that leads to a perfect job fit. The problem with accomplishments is that they tend to be discrete, anecdotal activities; they may or may not be significant indicators of more basic motivated behavioral patterns that affect your job performance. It's only when a *pattern* emerges from an analysis of your key accomplishments that we begin seeing the true power of this type of job search approach.

> **Ask Yourself**
>
> ☑ What really motivates me at work?
>
> ☑ How do other people view my work?
>
> ☑ What are my major strengths?
>
> ☑ Can I help employers hire my future?
>
> ☑ Is there something very unique about me?

This type of analysis is the basis for developing a savvy resume that clearly communicates your motivated pattern of behavior to employers. It's not just a pattern of behavior we're interested in; we want to know your *motivated* pattern of behavior. Savvy employers need to know what really turns you on—your passion at work or those things that motivate you to achieve great things.

Take, for example, these ten major accomplishments, or achievements, a candidate might identify as his most important accomplishments over a 15-year period. These are *motivated achievements*—those things he really did well and enjoyed doing:

- *Started a small paper route and within 3 years built it into the largest route in the district.*

- *Created a small paper recycling program amongst my customers that resulted in receiving the annual Junior Achievement Award for developing an innovative environmental care project.*

- *Earned 50 percent of my college expenses by designing Web pages and maintaining Web sites for fellow students.*

- *Completed my Master's degree within 18 months while working full-time.*

- *Organized a community benefit that raised over $50,000 to construct new camp facilities at Mason Ridge Park.*

- *Finished in the top 10 in the annual Washington-Baltimore Marathon.*

- *Served as the designer and general contractor for my new home which resulted in saving more than $35,000.*

- *Managed a complex construction project that was completed six weeks before deadline and resulted in the company receiving a $200,000 bonus for early project completion.*

- *Developed a new team approach to scheduling and supply chain management that resulted in (1) eliminating the use of outside consultants, (2) saving the company nearly $1 million a year, and (3) improving customer satisfaction by 30 percent with new on-time delivery of services.*

While each of these accomplishments is interesting with their focus on results, outcomes, or benefits, examined individually they tell you nothing about a possible motivated pattern of behavior that can predict future performance. Each could be a once-in-a-lifetime accomplishment that is neither sustainable nor predictable. But when examined together and analyzed for common characteristics, what emerges from these discrete accomplishments is a clear pattern of behavior that may continue into the future. In other words, it's a predictable motivated pattern of behavior. An analysis of these nine accomplishments might conclude the following about the "fitness" of this candidate:

This is a highly entrepreneurial, competitive, energetic, and confi-dent self-starter. He consistently takes initiative, assumes leader-ship roles, works well in team settings, challenges himself, and op-erates with the "big picture" in mind. He's used to getting things done in a timely fashion and moving on to new challenges. He likes to see concrete results that are directly attributed to his work.

In this case, knowing your accomplishments may impress the employer that you are a "doer," but these accomplishments alone don't tell the employer what kind of "consistent doer" you are. By knowing your pattern, the employer has a solid basis for predicting your behavior in his or her organization.

If an employer has a position that is designed around this particu-lar pattern of accomplishments, this person would most likely be a perfect "fit" for the job. However, if the position is designed for someone with a strong pattern of followership—completes projects on time, works well in team settings, quickly operationalizes management's goals—or if the organization is highly bureaucratic, with many layers of decision-making affecting individual perfor-mance, this individual might quickly get bored and soon begin look-ing elsewhere for a more challenging opportunity that best fits his behavioral profile. At the same time, this person might be a good candidate for changing the culture of the organization, especially if he were hired in a top-level position for re-engineering the organiza-tion in the direction of greater decentralization and entrepreneurism.

The point of this illustration is that, to a certain extent, work behavior is predictable if given the right tools for analyzing behav-ior. If an employer knows what your basic motivated pattern of work behavior is before hiring you, he or she can make a wise hiring deci-sion. If an employer only focuses on your past experiences related to performing formal duties and responsibilities—without knowing your predictable pattern of behavior—he or she is likely to make a hiring mistake. You can help employers avoid such mistakes by clearly communicating your motivated pattern of behavior on your resume as well as in job interviews. You do this by revealing what it is that makes you a perfect "fit" for the job—leaving less to the interpretation of the employer.

> You can help employers avoid hiring mistakes by clearly communicating your motivated pattern of behavior on your resume as well as in job interviews.

The Hierarchy of Motivated Behavior

It's useful to think of your motivated pattern of behavior as the top of a behavioral pyramid. Take, for example, the following figure:

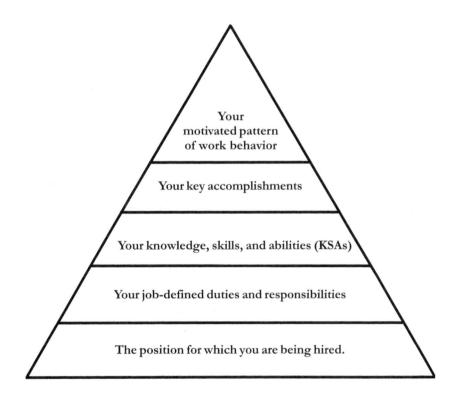

Your motivated pattern of work behavior

Your key accomplishments

Your knowledge, skills, and abilities (KSAs)

Your job-defined duties and responsibilities

The position for which you are being hired.

At the very base of this pyramid is the position for which you are being hired. Positions tend to be more or less well defined. Some positions lack clear definition; employers often let candidates define the position by purposefully defining it in very general terms.

Next come the duties and responsibilities that are assigned to the position. These elements often appear in job descriptions and are most prevalent on resumes of candidates who view a resume as a summary of one's work history.

What many employers focus on is the next level, the KSAs or the key knowledge, skills, and abilities that appear to be appropriate for performing the job that defines the position. They often outline the required KSAs for a position and then try to decipher if a candidate's experience, as profiled on a resume, includes those qualifying KSAs. Unfortunately, most resumes are mired in duties and responsibilities with scant attention given to basic KSAs. The federal government in particular has perfected the art of analyzing, writing, requiring, and reviewing candidates' KSAs. If a candidate's resume or application with the federal government fails to include appropriate KSAs, he or she will be passed over for consideration because they lack the necessary qualifiers. However, KSAs are just one step above formal duties and responsibilities. They raise the "qualifying bar" and thus eliminate hundreds of potential candidates at the initial review stage. In other words, they simplify the screening process. In the end, KSAs are not good predictors of future performance because they do not reveal a motivated pattern of behavior that is key to projecting future performance.

Your goal in the job search, and especially in writing a savvy resume, is to put yourself and employers at the top of our pyramid of behavior. Let potential employers know that you have a unique motivated pattern of work behavior supported by key accomplishments, that they should seriously consider in their deliberations. If they hire this motivated pattern, they will make a wise hiring decision. If you do this, you will be the applicant the employer "likes" the most!

Employer's Expectations

Employers have many expectations in today's job market. Their most important expectation is that they will hire the right person for the job and that person will contribute substantially to the continuing growth of their organization. But such expectations are often dashed because of the way employers and candidates conduct themselves in the job search/hiring situation. Employers, too, have patterns of behavior that may or may not be conducive to the health of their organizations. Many employers continue to make bad hiring decisions because they are poor judges of what they really should be hiring—predictable patterns of behavior rather than individuals associated with particular duties, responsibilities, and KSAs.

Indeed, savvy employers know they have made many hiring mistakes in the past. Just take a look at the suggestive titles of the most recent spate of books on hiring, retention, and job satisfaction issues:

- *45 Effective Ways For Hiring Smart*
- *96 Great Interview Questions to Ask Before You Hire*
- *Ask the Right Questions, Hire the Best People*
- *The Difficult Hire*
- *Don't Hire a Crook!*
- *Finding and Keeping Great Employees*
- *Getting Employees to Fall in Love With Your Company*
- *Hire With Your Head*
- *How to Be a Star At Work*
- *Love 'Em or Lose 'Em*
- *Smart Hiring*
- *Smart Staffing*

This is no coincidence that so many experts are now advising employers to change the way they have been hiring or pay the heavy costs attendant with high turnover and low worker morale. Savvy employers are determined not to repeat this pattern in the future. After all, hiring errors can be costly to an organization in terms of both direct replacement costs and lost opportunity costs. Such errors also affect the morale of others whose work is disrupted by such personnel changes. In fact, turnover and retention studies report that on average it costs $50,000 or more to replace an employee. Receiving an expensive wake-up call in today's economy, few employers can sustain such high replacement costs by repeating a pattern of bad hiring decisions. As a result, many of them are determined to correct their errors and literally "hire with their heads" by changing the way they initially screen resumes, test candidates, conduct interviews, and extend offers. They increasingly look for more predictable *behavioral clues* in candidates by doing the following:

1. **Scrutinize resumes more closely for clear patterns of accomplishments—the content of our behavioral resumes.** More and more employers scan resumes, use resume databases, and screen resumes by keywords. More and more keywords have behavioral content that go beyond traditional nouns that make up many "Keyword Summaries" on electronic resumes. "Professional Profiles," "Core Competencies," and "Summary of Achievements" play an increasingly important role in this screening process.

2. **Subject more and more candidates to achievement and psychological tests, behavioral profiling, and drug testing.** These screening tests are often administered immediately *before* a candidate interviews for a position. The results may eliminate a candidate from the

interview or they may be used during the job interview for asking probing questions about an individual's behavior or psychological predispositions. For example, if your test results show that you are a contemplative and analytical type—rather than a self-starter who enjoys taking a lot of initiative—but you are applying for a sales position, an employer may immediately conclude that you are not a good "fit" for this position. You'll have to explain, with examples of concrete accomplishments, why your particular pattern would work for this position. Chances are you will be quickly eliminated from consideration because your psychological predispositions and behavioral patterns will be perceived as inappropriate for the position. The employer knows this because study after study confirms that only one type of individual performs best in this position. Regardless of how likable you may be, you're simply not the type of person who will do well in this position. In fact, this employer does you a favor by immediately eliminating you from consideration based on such a test. It's what you should have done yourself—long before you wrote your resume and applied for the job. At the very minimum, you should have taken the *Myers-Briggs Type Indicator* and *Strong Interest Inventory*, which are widely administered by high schools, community colleges, and career professionals, to get a better understanding of yourself and the types of jobs that are best "fit" for you. You need to be looking for positions that best fit your particular psychological and behavioral profile.

3. **Conduct more and more interviews with a single candidate.** Rather than go to two or three interviews with a single employer, expect to encounter situations where you may go to five, six, or seven interviews, each being a new

type of interview (one-on-one, sequential, serial, panel, group) and involving a different number and level of participants. Not surprisingly, you may be exhausted after the fourth interview! But that's okay from the employer's perspective. Hiring is a risky and potentially expensive business that requires such thorough screening methods. Employers want to discover the "real you"—not some terrific role player who has practiced the latest canned answers to interview questions dished out by today's enterprising career writers. If done right, each of these interviews may tell an employer something new about your behavior and provide important insights into your potential "fit" with the organization.

4. **Scrutinize references more carefully by asking probing behavioral questions of previous employers.** Expect employers to ask your previous employer such things as these:

- *What were her three most important achievements during the past two years?*

- *Can you give me an example of how he took initiative in solving a major problem?*

- *What were some of her major weaknesses that she managed to correct?*

- *Can you give me an example of how he worked with other team members in meeting project deadlines?*

- *What five words would you use to predict her future performance?*

- *If you hired him again, what two changes would you like to see him make?*

In other words, more and more employers are taking reference checks seriously. They know they can gain valuable insights into a candidate's behavior—but only if they go beyond the superficial and ask the right questions.

5. **Negotiate lengthier probationary periods in order to see if the new hire indeed works out according to expectations.** Even though more and more employers focus on identifying motivated behaviors of candidates, hiring is still a risky business. The true test of whether or not a candidate is a good fit is on-the-job performance. Expect employers to build in three- and six- month probationary periods in order to thoroughly review your performance prior to accepting you as a permanent employee. It's during that period when employers get to see the "real you" at work and identify what should be your long-term motivated patterns of work behavior.

Employers who make hiring mistakes may end up paying for it in more ways than one. In today's competitive economy, few employers can afford making such mistakes. They increasingly seek good indicators of employee behavior. Therefore, it's incumbent upon you to meet and hopefully exceed their expectations by starting with a savvy resume that is rich in behavioral content.

Focus On the Unique You

Whatever you do, avoid producing a resume that looks like every other resume on the market today. Your goal should be to communicate the "unique you" rather than play the typical role of job applicant. You begin communicating this unique you in your resume and letters, in telephone conversations, and during face-to-face interviews. You exude a certain professional and personal style that makes you appear special in the eyes of employers—someone they want to hire. Let employers know what is so special about you. What exactly are your passions? What motivates or turns you on at work? Is it the nature of the work, the people you work with, or the challenge of working on interesting projects and accomplishing important goals? What types of things do you normally accomplish? How do you handle new challenges? Are you constantly learning new things and developing new skills to improve your performance and advance your career? Are you someone an employer can depend on for solving problems and getting things done? Are you a star performer who takes ownership of your job?

Once you identify your accomplishments and motivated pattern of behavior, you'll come face-to-face with your special standout qualities. You'll begin seeing a new "unique you" that should be communicated over and over to employers. When you communicate these qualities on your resume, yours will stand out from the crowd of other resumes that primarily focus on formal job titles, duties, and responsibilities. Your resume tells employers loudly and clearly that you have special qualities that make you a perfect fit for the job. You are someone who can hit the ground running and produce concrete results, just like you have done in previous jobs and other areas of your life.

Stress Your Key Accomplishments

Your accomplishments are the building blocks for identifying and communicating your motivated pattern of behavior. As we saw earlier in the chapter, when we examined and analyzed nine accomplishments, and which we will outline in greater depth when we focus on developing your resume objective in Chapter 5, your accomplishments provide important clues to what really turns you on. When you analyze your accomplishments, you begin seeing important patterns in your behavior. These patterns can be synthesized into a few key behaviors that become the basis for communicating the "unique you" to employers. You become known for what you will likely achieve in the future rather than what you did in the past. As you shift your focus from your work history to your probable future performance, as identified from your motivated pattern of behavior, you begin speaking the language of employers. Your accomplishments become the *supports* for communicating your future performance. Always remember, employers want to hire your future, not your past. They are less interested in where you worked and what you did last week or two years ago than what you will do for them next month, next year, or three years from now.

> When you analyze your accomplishments, you begin important patterns in your behavior. Employers want to hire your future rather than your past.

You should always focus on your accomplishments rather than on your duties and responsibilities. One of the best ways to do this is to keep a running list of your accomplishments, both minor and major. You really should be doing this anyway as part of your preparation for your company's ongoing performance appraisal process. Document what it is you have done particularly well and enjoyed doing. Once you have a comprehensive list of your accomplishments—ideally 100 or more accomplishments—you will have a rich database from which to formulate a resume objective and communicate your motivated pattern of behavior to employers.

Develop a Powerful Behavior-Based Resume

Our goal in the next few chapters is to make sure you produce a very different type of resume than you have in the past. We want you to communicate the "unique you" to employers—first in a resume and letters and then in job interviews. Indeed, your resume will become the basis for conducting an effective job search because it focuses everyone's attention around what you have done, can do, and will do in the future. As we analyze your accomplishments and build each section of your resume, you'll begin seeing the power of a behavior-based resume. You may even discover a "new you," someone who should be viewed as very special in the eyes of employers. You'll focus on your strengths rather than dwell on your weaknesses. Above all, you'll have a clear sense of direction and renewed purpose as you navigate today's job market in search of the perfect job that will fully utilize your talents as clearly identified in your motivated pattern of behavior.

4

THE SAVVY RESUME PROCESS

I
t's one thing to talk about the importance of a savvy resume and another to get down to the nuts and bolts of actually producing and marketing this type of resume. You'll need to first understand the process or steps involved in developing and communicating a savvy resume as well as find the time to write it and implement a plan of action involving production, distribution, and follow-up. Indeed, as you will quickly discover, this is not the type of resume you can throw together in a few hours. It requires lots of thoughtful analysis, several hours of writing, and a well-conceived plan of action.

A Seven-Step Process

So where do you start when writing a resume? Do you begin at the top (Objective) and work your way to the bottom (Personal Information) or start at the bottom and work toward the top? Should you first do what comes easiest (Work History) or tackle the big jobs first (Objective). The savvy resume writing process involves seven important steps, each of which should be completed in sequence. These steps are outlined in the figure on page 56 and summarized as follows:

7 - Step Savvy Resume Process

Identify motivated skills and abilities	**1**	
Specify a job/career objective	**2**	PREPARATION STEPS
Develop resume database	**3**	
Draft each section	**4**	
Finalize the savvy resume	**5**	WRITING STEPS
Produce the final resume	**6**	
Develop/implement a plan of action	**7**	ACTION STEPS

1. **Identify your motivated skills and abilities.** This is the very first thing everyone should do when preparing to conduct a job search—conduct a self-assessment. It's what we call "doing first things first"—identifying exactly who you are in terms of your interests, skills, abilities, and accomplishments. You can complete this step by taking professionally administered tests, such as the *Myers-Briggs Type Indicator* and *Strong Interest Inventory*, or completing several pencil and paper exercises as we identify in Chapter 5. The most important point here is that you must complete this step—the more thorough the better—*before* you do anything else with your resume. If you don't know who you really are in terms of your interests, skills, abilities, and accomplishments, chances are you will write a very weak and unfocused resume that either lacks an objective or includes a trite objective as well as emphasizes your work history, duties, and responsibilities. It will not give employers many clues as to what you are likely to do for them in the future.

   Ask Yourself

   ☑ What's the best way to write a resume?

   ☑ Am I a passive or proactive job seeker?

   ☑ Can I find enough time to be successful?

   ☑ Will I commit myself to becoming more proactive?

   ☑ Do I know where to find professional assistance?

2. **Specify a job or career objective.** We assume you have goals and many of them relate to your job and career. If you have trouble articulating your job and career goals, don't worry. This will all come together once you have had a chance to complete your self-assessment in Step 1. This can be the most time consuming step of all. It may

take you hours, even days, to come up with a very thought-ful and targeted 25-word objective that will appear at the very beginning of your resume. Your objective will give your resume and job search important direction.

3. **Develop a database for writing each resume section**. Before you begin writing each section of your resume, you need to outline in detail all possible information that could be included in each resume section. While you will not include all of the data on your resume—perhaps only 10 percent—at least you will have a large and systematic database to draw from in crafting each resume section. Take an inventory, for example, of your educational back-ground and work history as well as develop a comprehen-sive list of your accomplishments related to specific jobs. Use the forms in Chapter 5 to generate this database.

4. **Draft each section for appropriate elements and lan-guage.** You may need to write and rewrite your resume several times. The goal is to create a one- to two-page resume that is both a quick and powerful read. The lan-guage must be interesting and engaging. Each section must quickly flow into the next section. A savvy resume is one that has been edited and proofed several times. It has been subjected to ruthless revisions. It has been drafted and re-drafted several times—word for word, line by line, and section by section—until it becomes a powerful state-ment of your qualifications.

5. **Finalize the savvy resume.** The final draft involves at-tention to important visual presentation elements, such as layout, spacing, type style, and emphasizing techniques.

Here you make critical "dress for success" decisions concerning the overall visual impact of your resume. At the same time, you need to consider the fact that you may need to email your resume or that it may be scanned into a resume database—situations that require greater attention to special formats and the use of keywords.

6. **Produce the final product.** This step involves making decisions concerning how you will produce your resume. It concerns such things as selection of paper quality and color, printing equipment, and duplication methods.

7. **Develop and implement a plan of action.** Your plan of action encompasses two important implementation steps organized over a specific time frame: distribution and follow-up. How long do you expect to be sending out your resume to potential employers and others who might be able to assist you with your job search? Will this take place over an intense six-week period or during a leisurely six-month period? Who should receive your resume? How should you send it? Should you broadcast or only target it toward specific employers? When and how should you follow-up your resume? Which follow-up methods seem to work best? And don't forget what additional elements should accompany your resume, especially cover and follow-up letters. In other words, this final step in the savvy resume process emphasizes the fact that while resume writing and production are important, what really counts is implementation of an action plan. You must market your resume by getting it into the right hands and ensuring that it gets read and responded to. In the end, the effectiveness of a resume is largely determined by the

> The effectiveness of a resume is largely determined by the quality of one's distribution and follow-up methods. Neglect these points and you will be left with nothing more than a pretty resume that you may enjoy reading over and over to yourself.

quality of one's distribution and follow-up methods. Neglect the importance of distribution and follow-up and you will be left with nothing more than a pretty resume that you may enjoy reading over and over to yourself. Remember, a resume has purpose: generate invitations to job interviews. You can only get such invitations if you pay close attention to the details of implementation.

Finding More Proactive Time

Many job seekers suffer from one of life's great constraints—not enough time to do things right. They often understand the process, know what needs to be done, find enough time to create an acceptable resume, and then short-change the whole implementation process by devoting little time to distribution and follow-up. Instead of being proactive, they become passive participants—a spectator rather than a key player. They sit on the sidelines contemplating when they will "win" the job search game. With a resume in hand, and perhaps hoping to be struck by lightning, they do little to advance their job search because they claim to have little time to devote to those implementation activities that really count. They, in effect, sabotage their resume by not finding enough time to see the process through to the very end. As a result, many job seekers try to save time, and rationalize that they are indeed "doing something" about this situation, by spending most of their precious implementation time on relatively passive distribution activities: (1) sending their resume in response to classified ads, (2) broadcasting their resume to numerous employers, and (3) using the Internet to post their resume and seek out online vacancy announcements. What they most need is to find proactive time rather than carve out more passive job search time.

If you feel you have little proactive time to devote to implementing your job search, it may be time to assess your current use of time. Time management experts estimate that most people waste their time on unimportant matters. Lacking priorities, people spend 80 percent of their time on trivia and 20 percent of their time on the important matters that should get the most attention. If you reverse this emphasis, you could have a great deal of excess time—and probably experience less stress attendant with the common practice of crisis managing the critical 20 percent.

A realistic approach to better managing your time is to start monitoring your time use and then gradually reorganize your time according to goals and priorities. Start by developing a time management log that helps you monitor your present use of time. Keep daily records of how you use your time over a two week period. Identify who controls your time and the results of your time utilization. Within two weeks, clear patterns will emerge. You may learn that you have an "open door" policy that enables others to control your time, leaving little time to do your own work. Based on this information, you may need to close your door and be more selective about access. You may find from your analysis that you use most time for activities that have few, if any, important outcomes. If this is the case, then you may need to set goals and prioritize daily activities.

A simple yet effective technique for improving your time management practices is to complete a "to do" list for each day. This list also should prioritize which activities are most important to accomplish each day. Include at the top of your list a particular job search activity or several activities that should be completed on each day. If you follow this simple time management practice, you will find the necessary time to include your job search in your daily routines. You can give your job search top priority. Better still, you will accomplish more in less time, and with better results.

If you can set aside more quality time to devote to your job search, you may be amazed with the results of your distribution and follow-up activities. As you move from passive to proactive time, you'll begin seeing there is more to this process than being struck by lightning. You begin putting yourself in the right places and at the right time with a savvy resume that generates many invitations to job interviews. But you must first find more proactive time to make this process work properly.

Implementing a Plan

A typical job search takes anywhere from one month to six months, depending on a mix of several factors. Plan to spend at least three months of hard work looking for a job. It may take only a few weeks to make the right connections or it could take six months to successfully complete the process. Throughout the job search, you will be using your resume frequently to open doors for information, advice, referrals, and job interviews.

Assuming you have found more proactive time to devote to your job search, we also strongly recommend that you routinize many of your job search activities. One good way of doing this is to commit yourself in writing to achieving certain job search milestones as well as structuring weekly job search activities and monitoring weekly accomplishments. Use the two forms on pages 63 and 64 to develop such commitments. Make multiple copies of the "Weekly Job Performance and Planning Report" form on page 65 so you can complete one of these forms each week. If you use these forms together, the end result should be a self-monitored planning and evaluation system that forces you into a continuous proactive mode. It reminds you that success is a product of doing certain things over and over and over again with different individuals and groups. Coupled with

Job Search Contract

1. I'm committed to changing my life by changing my job. Today's date is _____.

2. I will manage my time so that I can successfully complete my job search and find a high quality job. I will begin changing my time management behavior on _____.

3. I will begin my job search on _____.

4. I will involve _____ with my job search.
   (individual/group)

5. I will spend at least one week conducting library research on different jobs, employers, and organizations. I will begin this research during the week of _____.

6. I will complete my skills identification step by _____.

7. I will complete my objective statement by _____.

8. I will complete my resume by _____.

9. Each week I will:
   - make _____ new job contacts.
   - conduct _____ informational interviews.
   - follow-up on _____ referrals.

10. My first job interview will take place during the week of _____.

11. I will begin my new job by _____.

12. I will make a habit of learning one new skill each year.

Signature: _____

Date: _____

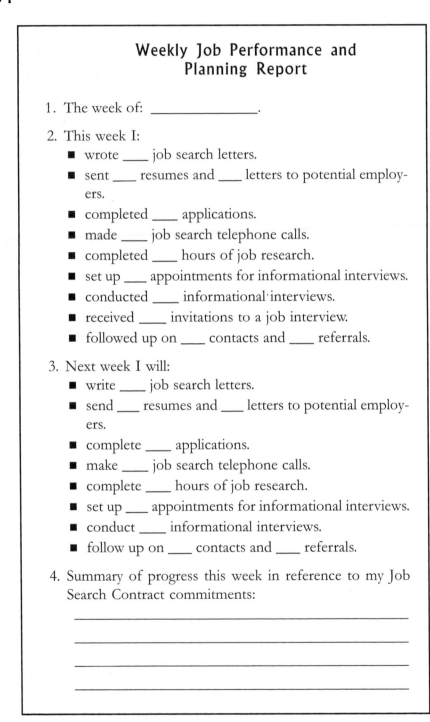

Weekly Job Performance and Planning Report

1. The week of: _____.

2. This week I:
   - wrote ____ job search letters.
   - sent ____ resumes and ____ letters to potential employ-ers.
   - completed ____ applications.
   - made ____ job search telephone calls.
   - completed ____ hours of job research.
   - set up ____ appointments for informational interviews.
   - conducted ____ informational·interviews.
   - received ____ invitations to a job interview.
   - followed up on ____ contacts and ____ referrals.

3. Next week I will:
   - write ____ job search letters.
   - send ____ resumes and ____ letters to potential employ-ers.
   - complete ____ applications.
   - make ____ job search telephone calls.
   - complete ____ hours of job research.
   - set up ____ appointments for informational interviews.
   - conduct ____ informational interviews.
   - follow up on ____ contacts and ____ referrals.

4. Summary of progress this week in reference to my Job Search Contract commitments:

   _____

   _____

   _____

   _____

your new time management practices, you *will* find the necessary time to do the job search properly. Most important of all, you *will* be in a constant proactive mode doing things that count the most for achieving job search success.

Seek Professional Assistance If Necessary

Many job seekers can conduct a job search on their own. They pick up a book, such as this one, and put it into practice with success. However, many other job seekers could benefit greatly from working with a career professional throughout the whole job search process or during certain critical stages of the process. A professional can provide needed expertise, from testing to interview preparation. Most important of all, an experienced and competent career professional provides both structure and support—he or she, in effect, becomes your personal coach—to help you see the process through to the end. Organizations, such as Bernard Haldane Associates (*www.jobhunting.com*), maintain a network of over 80 offices in the United States, Canada, and the United Kingdom, to assist individuals with their job search. For more information on their approach and offices, see their three new job search books: *Haldane's Best Resumes For Professionals, Haldane's Best Cover Letters For Professionals,* and *Haldane's Best Answers to Tough Interview Questions.* Many other career professionals can be found through your community college or through a network of counselors in private practice. Your community college is an especially good place to contact for taking two key baseline assessment tests, the Myers-Briggs Type Indicator and the Strong Interest Inventory. Other good starting points for finding someone to assist you would be an adult education program, high school guidance counselors, a women's center or local or county government programs. All of these places can put you in contact with the right people.

Whatever you do, make sure you do your job search right which means putting together a savvy resume. If you have difficulty doing this on your own, by all means seek professional assistance. It may or may not be expensive, but the structure and support you receive from a professional can be invaluable. A professional can help shorten your job search time, get you through the occasional psychological ups and downs associated with these activities, and help you move into a much higher paying position that more than off-sets the costs of their services. In other words, don't be "penny-wise but pound foolish" with your future by always trying to do it on your own.

Use this and other job search books to help you decide what type of services you need and to utilize them to the fullest extent by speaking the language of the professional. You'll be a smart user of such services—and may find you are motivated to do it on your own—if you first complete this book to the best of your abilities.

5

SAVVY WRITING

The structure of a savvy resume should include several key elements that relate to a well-conceived combination or hybrid resume. Each of these elements follows certain principles centered on developing a database and writing each section according to guidelines appropriate for behavior-based resumes. The end product of these data-gathering and writing activities should be a savvy resume that clearly communicates who you are in terms of your motivated patterns of behavior. It will include *supports*, or examples of accomplishments, that will most likely be the basis for structuring behavior-based interviews. This type of resume, in effect, will help structure the job interview by setting an agenda of behavior-based questions in your favor. In other words, a savvy resume is both employer-centered and candidate-centered.

Combination or Hybrid Resumes

Above all, a savvy resume is a combination or hybrid resume. In contrast to two other prevalent types of resumes—chronological and functional—this type of resume focuses on goals, skills, and accomplishments rather than on chronology of work experience (chronological resume) or action verbs and pithy phrases descriptive of soft interpersonal and workplace skills (functional resume). We find chronological and functional resumes to be inappropriate for most job search situations. They are weak resumes that do not showcase much behavioral content in candidates. Regardless of their so-called advantages and disadvantages, chronological and functional resumes should be avoided. They are antithetical to the hiring and employability needs of both employers and employees in today's talent-driven economy.

Structure of Resume Elements

A savvy resume should include certain structural elements normally associated with combination or hybrid resumes. As illustrated on page 67, these include six or seven major elements:

1. Contact information
2. Objective
3. Summary of Qualifications or Core Competencies
4. Achievements
5. Experience or Work History
6. Education
7. Optional personal statement

We'll address each of these elements later in this chapter. For now, let's think in terms of presenting your "qualifications" according to this structure of elements. The basic organizing principle is to always put the most important information first. If, for example, you are first entering the job market with little work experience, but your education is one of your major qualifications, you may want to move "Education" near the beginning of your resume.

RESUME STRUCTURE

Name
Street Address
City, State, Zip
Phone Numbers

OBJECTIVE: _____

_____

SUMMARY OF QUALIFICATIONS: _____

_____

_____

ACHIEVEMENTS: _____

_____

_____

_____

_____

EXPERIENCE:
Title/Company _____

_____

_____ Date

Title/Company _____

_____

_____ Date

EDUCATION: _____

_____

_____ Date

Develop a Comprehensive Database

Your writing plan should first begin with developing a comprehensive database from which to distill the most important information to include on your resume. Begin by completing the worksheets on pages 71–76. You may need to make multiple copies of the "Experience" and "Military" worksheets on pages 71–72, depending on the extent of your work experience. The most important sections on these worksheets relate to your significant contributions and achievements and demonstrated skills and abilities. These are the key building blocks for developing the behavioral focus on your savvy resume.

Focus on Your Motivated Accomplishments

After you've completed these worksheets, begin focusing on your accomplishments or achievements. Ideally, you should outline a list of 100 or more accomplishments. While many of them appear on the various worksheets you just completed, others may relate to other types of activities. They may go back to things you did as a youth. You especially want to focus on your motivated accomplishments— anything you did particularly well and enjoyed doing. Remember, in our example in Chapter 3, we identified a list of nine such accomplishments for one individual, which are worth revisiting here as we build each resume section:

- *Started a small paper route and within 3 years built it into the largest route in the district.*

- *Created a small paper recycling program amongst my customers that resulted in receiving the annual Junior Achievement Award for developing an innovative environmental care project.*

EMPLOYMENT EXPERIENCE WORKSHEET

1. Name of employer: _____

2. Address: _____

   _____

3. Inclusive dates of employment: From_____to _____.

month/year   month/year

4. Type of organization: _____

5. Size of organization/approximate number of employees: _____

6. Approximate annual sales volume or annual budget: _____

7. Position held: _____

8. Earnings per month/year: _____

9. Responsibilities/duties: _____

   _____

   _____

   _____

10. Achievements or significant contributions: _____

    _____

    _____

11. Demonstrated skills and abilities: _____

    _____

    _____

12. Reason(s) for leaving: _____

    _____

MILITARY EXPERIENCE WORKSHEET

1. **Service:** _____

2. **Rank:** _____

3. **Inclusive dates:** From_____ to _____.

                           month/year   month/year

4. **Responsibilities/duties:** _____

   _____

   _____

   _____

   _____

5. **Significant contributions/achievements:** _____

   _____

   _____

   _____

   _____

   _____

6. **Demonstrated skills and abilities:** _____

   _____

   _____

   _____

   _____

   _____

7. **Reserve status:** _____

COMMUNITY/CIVIC/ VOLUNTEER EXPERIENCE

1. Name and address of organization/group: _____

   _____

   _____

   _____

2. Inclusive dates: From_____to_____.

                  month/year   month/year

3. Offices held/nature of involvement: _____

   _____

   _____

   _____

4. Significant contributions/achievements/projects: _____

   _____

   _____

   _____

   _____

   _____

5. Demonstrated skills and abilities: _____

   _____

   _____

   _____

   _____

EDUCATIONAL DATA

1. **Institution:** _____

2. **Address:** _____

   _____

3. **Inclusive dates:** From _____ to _____.

                                month/year   month/year

4. **Degree or years completed:** _____

5. **Major(s):** _____ **Minor(s):** _____

6. **Education highlights:** _____

   _____

   _____

7. **Student activities:** _____

   _____

   _____

8. **Demonstrated abilities and skills:** _____

   _____

   _____

9. **Significant contributions/achievements:** _____

   _____

   _____

   _____

10. **Special training courses:** _____

    _____

11. **G.P.A.:** _____ (on _____ index)

                   point

ADDITIONAL INFORMATION

1. **Professional memberships and status:**

    a. _____

    b. _____

    c. _____

    d. _____

2. **Licenses/certifications:**

    a. _____

    b. _____

    c. _____

3. **Expected salary range:** $ _____ to $_____ (but do not include this on your resume)

4. **Acceptable amount of on-the-job travel:** _____ days per month.

5. **Areas of acceptable relocation:**

    a. _____   c. _____

    b. _____   d. _____

6. **Date of availability:** _____

7. **Contacting present employer:**
    a. Is he or she aware of your prospective job change? _____
    b. May he or she be contacted at this time? _____

8. **References:** (name, address, and telephone number—not to appear on resume)

    a. _____   c. _____

    b. _____   d. _____

9. **Foreign languages and degree of competency:**

   a. _____

   b. _____

10. **Interests and activities:** hobbies, avocations, and pursuits

    a. _____

    b. _____

    c. _____

    d. _____

    Circle letter of ones that support your objective.

11. **Foreign travel:**

Country	Purpose	Dates
a. _____	_____	_____
b. _____	_____	_____
c. _____	_____	_____

12. **Special awards/recognition:**

a. _____	_____	_____
b. _____	_____	_____
c. _____	_____	_____

13. **Special abilities/skills/talents/accomplishments:**

a. _____	_____	_____
b. _____	_____	_____
c. _____	_____	_____

- *Earned 50 percent of my college expenses by designing Web pages and maintaining Web sites for fellow students.*

- *Completed my Master's degree within 18 months while working full-time.*

- *Organized a community fundraising event that raised over $50,000 to construct new camp facilities at Mason Ridge Park.*

- *Finished in the top 10 in the annual Washington-Baltimore Marathon.*

- *Served as the designer and general contractor for my new home which resulted in saving more than $35,000.*

- *Managed a complex construction project that was completed six weeks before deadline and resulted in the company receiving a $200,000 bonus for early project completion.*

- *Developed a new team approach to scheduling and supply chain management that resulted in (1) eliminating the use of outside consultants, (2) saving the company nearly $1 million a year, and (3) improving customer satisfaction by 30 percent with new on-time delivery of services.*

The end result of analyzing these nine accomplishments was to characterize the individual as having this unique motivated behavioral pattern (MBP):

> *This is a highly entrepreneurial, competitive, energetic, and confident self-starter. He consistently takes initiative, assumes leadership roles, works well in team settings, challenges himself, and operates with the "big picture" in mind. He's used to getting things done in a timely fashion and moving on to new challenges. He likes to see concrete results that are directly attributed to his work.*

If you have difficulty identifying similar types of accomplishments, complete the following "Success Factor Analysis" exercise for identifying your major accomplishments. Yielding some of the most systematic and thorough data on individual accomplishments and patterns of motivated behavior, this exercise is widely used by professional career counselors and is sometimes referred to as the "System to Identify Motivated Skills" or "Intensive Skills Identification." Initially developed by Bernard Haldane Associates, each year this technique assists thousands of individuals in making job and career changes that are compatible with their MAS (motivated abilities and skills) or in the case of our savvy resume, your MBP (motivated behavioral pattern). Consisting of six progressive steps, this exercise will go a long way in helping you identify your unique MBP:

1. **Identify 15-20 accomplishments:** While ideally you should be able to list 100 to 150 one-sentence achievements or accomplishments (the richer the mix of achievements the better), let's start by focusing on a minimum of 15-20 accomplishments. These consist of things you enjoyed doing, believe you did well, and felt a sense of satisfaction, pride, or accomplishment in doing. You can see yourself performing at your best and enjoying your experiences when you analyze your accomplishments. This information reveals your *motivations* since it deals entirely with your voluntary behavior. In addition, it identifies what is right with you by focusing on your positives and strengths. You do this by identifying accomplishments throughout your life, beginning with your childhood. Your accomplishments should relate to specific experiences— not general ones—and may be drawn from work, leisure, education, military, or home life. Put each accomplishment at the top of a separate sheet of paper. Use the

above list of accomplishments as examples of what should appear at the top of each sheet of paper.

2. **Prioritize your ten most significant achievements.**

1. _____
2. _____
3. _____
4. _____
5. _____
6. _____
7. _____
8. _____
9. _____
10. _____

3. **Write a full page on each of your prioritized accomplishments.** You should describe:

   - How you initially became involved.

   - The details of *what you did* and *how you did it.*

   - What was especially enjoyable or satisfying to you.

   Use copies of the "Detailing Your Accomplishments" form on page 80 to outline your achievements.

4. **Elaborate on your accomplishments:** Have one or two other people interview you. For each accomplishment, have them note on a separate sheet of paper any terms used to reveal your skills, abilities, and personal qualities. To elaborate details, the interviewer(s) may ask:

DETAILING YOUR ACCOMPLISHMENTS

ACCOMPLISHMENT #_____ : _____

_____

_____

1. How did I initially become involved? _____

_____

_____

_____

_____

2. What did I do? _____

_____

_____

_____

_____

3. How did I do it? _____

_____

_____

_____

4. What was especially enjoyable about doing it? _____

_____

_____

_____

_____

- What was involved in the accomplishment?

- What was your part?

- What did you actually do?

- How did you go about that?

Clarify any vague areas by providing an example of what you did. Probe with the following questions:

- Would you elaborate with at least one example of what you mean?

- Could you give me an illustration?

- What were you good at doing?

This interview should clarify the details of your activities by asking only "what" and "how" questions. It should take 45 to 90 minutes to complete. Make copies of the "Strength Identification Interview" form on page 82 to guide you through this interview.

5. **Identify patterns by examining the interviewer's notes:** Together identify the recurring skills, abilities, and personal qualities *demonstrated* in your achievements. Search for *patterns*. Your MBP should become clear at this point; you should feel comfortable with it. If you have questions, review the data. If you disagree with a conclusion, disregard it. The results must accurately and honestly reflect how you operate.

6. **Synthesize the information by clustering similar skills into categories:** For example, your skills might be grouped in the following manner:

STRENGTH IDENTIFICATION INTERVIEW

Interviewee _____   Interviewer _____

INSTRUCTIONS: For each accomplishment, identify the **skills and abilities** the achiever actually demonstrated. Obtain details of the experience by asking *what* was involved with the achievement and *how* the individual made the achievement happen. Avoid "why" questions which tend to mislead. Ask for examples or illustrations of what and how.

Accomplishment #1:

Accomplishment #2:

Accomplishment #3:

Recurring abilities and skills:

Synthesized Skill Clusters

Investigate/Survey/Read Inquire/Probe/Question	Teach/Train/Drill Perform/Show/Demonstrate
Learn/Memorize/Practice Evaluate/Appraise/Assess Compare	Construct/Assemble/Put together
	Organize/Structure/Provide definition/Plan/Chart course Strategize/Coordinate
Influence/Involve/Get participation/Publicize Promote	Create/Design/Adapt/Modify

This exercise yields a relatively comprehensive inventory of your motivated skills and abilities. The information will better enable you to use a *MBP vocabulary* when identifying your objective, writing your resume and letters, and interviewing. Your self-confidence and self-esteem should increase accordingly!

Other MBP Alternatives

Several other techniques also can help you identify your motivated abilities and skills:

1. **List all of your hobbies.** Analyze what you do in each, which ones you like the most, what skills you use, and your most satisfying accomplishments.

2. **Conduct a job analysis** by writing about your past jobs and identifying which skills you used in each job. Cluster the skills into related categories and prioritize them according to your preferences.

3. **Purchase a copy of** Richard N. Bolles' *The New Quick Job Hunting Map, What Color Is Your Parachute?,* or *The Three Boxes of Life* (all from Ten Speed Press) and complete the lengthy "Map" exercise which is replicated in each of these publications.

4. **Acquire a copy of** Arthur F. Miller and Ralph T. Mattson's *The Truth About You* (Ten Speed Press) and work through the exercises found in the Appendix. While its overt religious message, extreme deterministic approach, and laborious exercises may turn off some users, you may find this book useful nonetheless. This is an abbreviated version of the authors' SIMA (System for Identifying Motivated Abilities) technique used by their career counseling firm, People Management, Inc. (924 First Street, Suite A, Snohomish, WA 98290, Tel. 206/563-0105). If you need professional assistance, contact this firm directly. They can provide you with several alternative services consistent with our MAS and MBP concepts.

5. **Complete John Holland's** *"The Self-Directed Search."* You'll find it in his book, *Making Vocational Choices: A Theory of Vocational Personalities and Work Environments* or in a separate publication entitled *The Self-Directed Search—A Guide to Educational and Vocational Planning.*

State an Employer-Centered Objective

You need to develop an employer-centered objective that will serve as the central organizing element at the very beginning of your resume. For us, putting an objective on a savvy resume is a non-issue. Without an objective, both you and your resume lacks critical focus and thus you may appear rudderless—you really don't appear to know what you want to do other than get a job that benefits you. By default, you'll probably create a reverse chronological resume (an obituary, work history driven resume) simply because you don't know what you want to do. If developed properly, an objective brings *focus* to both your resume and your job search. And it is a lack of focus that often results in a weak and haphazard job search.

Writing an employer-centered objective may be the most difficult part of the resume writing experience. Based on an analysis of your MBP, you should be able to clearly see where you have been coming from and where you are most likely to be going. In other words, your objective is not based on wishful thinking; it comes from a sound analysis of who you are in terms of your motivated skills and abilities. You examine your *pattern* and then project it into the future in relationship to the needs of employers (an employer-centered objective) rather than in reference to your needs (a self-centered objective). Examples of trite self-centered objectives you should avoid include:

A challenging position that leads to career advancement.

A position in Technical Sales with a progressive firm.

A training position that leads to rapid advancement.

If you select these types of objectives, you may be better off excluding an objective altogether on your resume! These objectives say nothing other than that you are probably a self-centered individual who may eat up the employer's bottom line—you want a good paying job that gives you even more money in the future as you climb the employer's advancement ladder. You appear to be an ambitious "careerist"—oriented toward position, money, and benefits; you probably have a sense of entitlement that may have a negative affect on co-workers. You'll probably leave your next employer for greener pastures as soon as your climb up the ladder slows. Some applicants also take this self-centered perspective into the job interview by asking questions about salary, benefits, and future advancement—just what employers like to hear from potential new hires! These objectives tell employers nothing about what you will do for them in the future, which is why they are considering you for a position in the first place.

Let's put this discussion within the framework of a powerful savvy resume. You need to develop an employer-centered objective that relates your MPB to the needs of employers as defined as possible *outcomes, results, or benefits*. This type of objective tells potential employers what really motivates you in terms of your interests, skills, and work. At your very professional core, this is what you really do well and enjoy doing—your key accomplishments. Take, for example, these two savvy resume objectives:

> *A challenging Public Relations position involving persuasive public speaking skills for promoting major publicity/ promotion campaigns relating to new product development.*

> *A entrepreneurial position using skills in* **Financial Analysis, Security Analysis, Budget Analysis,** *and* **Investment Strategies** *that will:*

> - *strengthen a company's financial position*
> - *identify new investment opportunities*
> - *develop effective financial strategies*
> - *forecast and manage future performance*

These are savvy resume objectives because they (1) are employer-centered, and (2) focus on core skills or competencies and possible outcomes related to one's MBP. They clearly communicate to potential employers that this is what really motivates the applicant—those things he does well and enjoys doing as well as the benefits he is prepared to give the employer. Most important of all, they subliminally pose the obvious question that takes the savvy resume writer to the next job search stage—the interview: *Can we talk about how my pattern of accomplishments relates to your needs?* The remainder of these individual's resumes provides *supports* for the employer-centered objectives. The supports are found in the next three resume sections: Qualifications Summary or Core Competencies, Achievements or Accomplishments, and Professional Experience.

Include a Qualifications Summary

Your Qualifications Summary, in effect, becomes a keyword summary on your major skills and core competencies. Take, for example, the individual whose objective focuses on Financial Analysis, Security Analysis, Budget Analysis, and Investment Strategies. His Qualifications Summary includes these core competencies that also serve as a rich compilation of keywords, or buzz words, of his profession:

QUALIFICATIONS SUMMARY

Over 8 years of progressive responsibility and expertise in financial environments with major achievements in the areas of:

• Financial Analysis/Planning	• Investment Analysis	• Financial Statement
• Strategic Planning	• E-Commerce	• Managerial Accounting
• Financial Management	• Cash Management	• Budget Analysis
• Risk Management	• Project Management	• Business Analysis
• Credit Analysis	• Business Valuation	• Acquisitions & Mergers

---

Another way to organize a powerful Qualifications Summary, which is less keyword-oriented, is as follows:

SUMMARY OF QUALIFICATIONS

- Fifteen years experience in office supervision and personnel management
- Highly motivated self-starter with aptitude for solving system problems
- Proficient in the use of the latest software programs, including Microsoft Word, PowerPoint, Excel, and Access
- Skilled in linking performance evaluation systems to career development programs

Another less conventional but still impressive way of presenting core competencies in a summary manner is to highlight one's expertise—presented as key accomplishments—in a particular professional position:

SENIOR PERSONNEL MANAGER
Turn-around Specialist and Senior Manager

Dynamic, creative, and results-oriented professional successful in developing model supervisory and personnel management systems for small businesses involved in restructuring their core manufacturing operations. Talented in custom-designing performance evaluation systems that dramatically increase employee satisfaction and retention as well as minimize recruitment and training costs.

Stress Your Key Accomplishments

This section includes a summary of your major accomplishments, achievements, or core competencies as they relate to the previous two resume sections—Objective and Summary of Qualifications. Try to list at least five major accomplishments that emphasizes results, outcomes, or benefits for employers and their clients. Taking again our example of the finance candidate, his first two accomplishments might appear as follows:

ACHIEVEMENTS

MANAGED the financial operation of a government contractor with $15 million in assets and $25 million in annual revenues. Provided complete leadership over accounting, payroll, banking, and risk management functions. **Results:** Saved employer over $500,000 in disallowed costs and significantly improved the company's financial position as a prerequisite for renewing a $12 million government contract.

DEVELOPED new e-commerce initiative for strengthening current customer base and for expanding telecommunication products into new global markets. **Results:** Increased online sales from $0 to $718,000 within the first six months of operation, followed by 25 percent increases in sales during each of the next three quarters.

Briefly Summarize Your Professional Experience

This section of your resume is very straightforward and probably the quickest and easiest to produce. Your Professional Experience basically becomes a summary of your Work History. Just briefly identify your employer, position, and inclusive employment dates. Since you've already presented your accomplishments in terms of results, it's not necessary to identify and embellish assigned duties and responsibilities associated with each position, however tempting and easy to do. Such information tells employers nothing about what you accomplished in terms of actual results, outcomes, or benefits. Simply state your work history as follows:

PROFESSIONAL EXPERIENCE

Allied Martin Systems, Inc.
Controller   1997 to present

Thompson Wales Consultants
Senior Accountant   1993–1996

Highlight Your Education

Education is another category you can quickly summarize, unless you have some extraordinary educational achievements that warrant special attention because they strengthen your Objective. The normal presentation of Education would appear as follows:

EDUCATION

| University of Illinois | MBA, Finance | 1997 |
| Vanderbilt University | BA, Accounting | 1989 |

If your education warrants special attention for reinforcing your Objective, you might consider embellishing it as follows:

EDUCATION

University of Illinois   MBA, Finance   1997
- Developed award-winning e-commerce business model for teaching undergraduate students
- Interned with Arthur Andersen as Investment Analyst

Vanderbilt University   BA, Accounting   1991
- Graduated with Honors, 3.8/4.0
- Worked full-time in earning 100% of educational and personal expenses

---

Consider Additional Information

You may want to end your resume after education. However, in some situations you may want to include additional information, such as special skills, professional affiliations, and personal statements. Again, only do this if this information strengthens your Objective. For example, if you are a high-energy person who seeks a high-energy, risk-taking, and mobile position, you might want to include the following "Personal" or "Interests" statements to reinforce the fact that your personal and professional lives encompass similar passions:

PERSONAL

• Willing to travel   • Tennis   • Deep Sea Fishing   • Hiking

---

or

INTERESTS

• Martial Arts   • Scuba Diving   • Hang Gliding   • Roller Blading

---

If you have special computer skills you wish to showcase, include them in a special "Computer Skills" section, like this:

COMPUTER SKILLS

• Microsoft Word   • Excel   • Access   • Windows   • PowerPoint
• PageMaker   • PhotoShop   • Lotus Notes

You also might want to include a special "Memberships and Affiliations" sector, such as this:

Memberships & Affiliations

- Society of Female Executives   • Society of Human Resource Management
- National Association of Trainers • Toastmasters International

---

If space permits, and you have taken the Myers-Briggs Type Indicator (MBTI) test, you may want to summarize your key interpersonal traits using the MBTI language. Also, consider including a section with positive comments about your accomplishments from former employers, co-workers, and clients. Such personal statements add a nice tough for re-emphasizing your patterns of behavior.

Put It All Together

Once you've drafted each section of your resume, put it together so it is one or two pages in length. While some resumes may run three to four pages, you're well advised to keep it to two pages, especially if you have over five years of work experience. Resumes that go beyond two pages often lose the reader's attention. When dealing with the issue of length, always remember the purpose of your resume: to get a job interview. Also, keep in mind that few resume readers really read resumes in depth—they tend to quickly *scan* resumes for buzz words, key skills, and statements of results. Indeed, few people spend more than 20 to 30 seconds scanning a resume—only enough time to at best get the jist of the resume. Not surprisingly, the person scanning your resume is most likely to be a very busy person who simply does not have much quality reading time. A well con-

> Resumes that go beyond two pages often lose the reader's attention. Few readers really read resumes in depth—they tend to quickly scan them for buzz words, key skills, and statements of results. Few spend more than 20 to 30 seconds scanning a resume.

ceived one- to two-page resume, organized with a clear objective and the most important information placed up front, is more likely to grab the attention of the reader and motivate him or her to respond to you with an invitation to a job interview.

Evaluate the Final Product

Once you've finish putting together each resume section, you should then conduct two types of evaluations: internal and external. These evaluations will give you useful feedback on improving every element in your resume as you go about re-drafting it into a final form. Start with the following 47 internal evaluation criteria:

INTERNAL RESUME EVALUATION

INSTRUCTIONS: Examine your resume writing skills in reference to the following evaluation criteria. Respond to each statement by circling the appropriate number to the right that most accurately describes your resume:

1 = Strongly Agree	4 = Disagree
2 = Agree	5 = Strongly Disagree
3 = So-So (Neutral)	

1. Wrote the resume myself—no creative plagiarizing from others' resume examples.　　1 2 3 4 5

2. Conducted a thorough self-assessment of my skills and accomplishments, which resulted in a clear motivated behavioral pattern (MBP) which became the basis for writing each resume section.　　1 2 3 4 5

3. Have a plan of action that relates my resume to other job search activities.　　1 2 3 4 5

4. Selected the combination or hybrid resume format for showcasing my pattern of accomplishments.　　1 2 3 4 5

5. Included all essential information categories in the strongest order to showcase my education, experience, and accomplishments.　　1 2 3 4 5

6. Eliminated all extraneous information unrelated to my objective and employers' needs (date, picture, race, religion, political affiliation, age, sex, height, weight, marital status, health, hobbies, salary history, references).　　1 2 3 4 5

7. Always put most important information first.　　1 2 3 4 5

8. Resume is oriented to the future rather than to the past.　　1 2 3 4 5

9. Included complete contact information— name, address, phone and fax numbers, email. No P.O. Box numbers or nicknames.　　1 2 3 4 5

10. Limited abbreviations to accepted words.　　1 2 3 4 5

11. Contact information attractively formatted to introduce the resume.　　1 2 3 4 5

12. Included a thoughtful employer-oriented objective that incorporates both skills and benefits.　　1 2 3 4 5

13. Objective clearly communicates to employers what I want to do, can do, and will do for them.　　1 2 3 4 5

14. Objective is neither too general nor too specific.　　　1　2　3　4　5

15. Objective serves as the central organizing element for all other sections of the resume.　　　1　2　3　4　5

16. Included a powerful "Summary of Qualifications," "Core Competencies," or "Professional Profile" section immediately following the "Objective."　　　1　2　3　4　5

17. Elaborated work experience in detail, emphasizing my skills, abilities, and accomplishments.　　　1　2　3　4　5

18. Each "Experience" section is short and to the point.　　　1　2　3　4　5

19. Consistently used action verbs and the active voice.　　　1　2　3　4　5

20. Did not refer to myself as "I."　　　1　2　3　4　5

21. Used specifics—numbers and percentages—to highlight the results of my achievements.　　　1　2　3　4　5

22. Included positive quotations about my performance from previous employers.　　　1　2　3　4　5

23. Eliminated any negative references, including reasons for leaving.　　　1　2　3　4　5

24. Does not include names of supervisors or others involved with my professional or personal life.　　　1　2　3　4　5

25. Listed my most recent job and then included other jobs in reverse chronological order.　　　1　2　3　4　5

26. Descriptions of "Experience" or "Achievements" are consistent.   1 2 3 4 5

27. Put the most important information on my skills first when summarizing my "Experience."   1 2 3 4 5

28. No time gaps nor "job hopping" apparent to reader.   1 2 3 4 5

29. Documented "other experience" that might strengthen my objective and decided to either include or exclude it on the resume.   1 2 3 4 5

30. Included complete information on my educational background, including important highlights.   1 2 3 4 5

31. If a recent graduate with little relevant work experience, emphasized educational background more than work experience.   1 2 3 4 5

32. Put education in reverse chronological order and eliminated high school if a college graduate.   1 2 3 4 5

33. Included special education and training relevant to my major interests and skills.   1 2 3 4 5

34. Included professional affiliations and membership relevant to my objective and skills; highlighted any major contributions.   1 2 3 4 5

35. Documented any special skills not included elsewhere on resume and included those that appear relevant to employers' needs.   1 2 3 4 5

36. Included awards or special recognition that further document my skills and achievements.   1 2 3 4 5

37. Weighed pros and cons of including a Personal Statement on my resume. 1 2 3 4 5

38. Did not mention salary history or expectations. 1 2 3 4 5

39. Did not include names, addresses, and phone number of references. 1 2 3 4 5

40. Included additional information to enhance the interest of employers. 1 2 3 4 5

41. Used a language appropriate for the employer, including terms that associate me with the industry. 1 2 3 4 5

42. Incorporated a crisp, succinct, expressive, and direct language. 1 2 3 4 5

43. Used highlighting and emphasizing techniques to make the resume most readable. 1 2 3 4 5

44. Resume has an inviting, uncluttered look, incorporating sufficient white space and using a standard type style and size. 1 2 3 4 5

45. Kept the design basic and conservative. 1 2 3 4 5

46. Kept sentences short and succinct. 1 2 3 4 5

47. Resume runs one or two pages. 1 2 3 4 5

TOTAL

Add the numbers you circled to the right of each statement to get a cumulative score. If your score is higher than 85, you need to work on improving various aspects of your resume. Do another draft of your resume and then re-evaluate it according to the same criteria.

You also should conduct an **external evaluation** of your resume by circulating it to three or more individuals. For guidelines, give your evaluators the form on page 33. Choose people whose opinions are objective, frank, and thoughtful. Do not select friends and relatives who usually flatter you with positive comments. Professional acquaintances or people you don't know personally but whom you admire may be good evaluators. An ideal evaluator has experience in hiring people in your area of job interest. In addition to sharing their experience with you, they may refer you to other individuals who would be interested in your qualifications. If you choose such individuals to critique your resume, ask them for their frank reaction—not what they would politely say to a candidate presenting such a resume. You want the people to role play with you—a potential interview candidate. Ask your evaluators:

If you don't mind, would you look over my resume? Perhaps you could comment on its clarity or make suggestions for improving it?

How would you react to this resume if you received it from a candidate? Would it grab your attention and interest you enough to interview?

If you were writing this resume, what changes would you make? Any additions, deletions, modifications?

You will normally receive good cooperation and advice by approaching people in this manner. In addition, you will probably get valuable unsolicited advice on other job search matters, such as job leads, job market information, and employment strategies.

Taken together, the internal and external evaluations should complement each other by providing you with maximum information for revising your draft resume.

EXTERNAL EVALUATION

INSTRUCTIONS: Circle the number that best characterizes various aspects of my resume. Please include any recommendations on how I could best improve the resume:

1 = Excellent   2 = Okay   3 = Weak

**Recommendations
For Improvement**

1. Overall appearance	1	2	3	_____
2. Layout	1	2	3	_____
3. Clarity	1	2	3	_____
4. Consistency	1	2	3	_____
5. Readability	1	2	3	_____
6. Language	1	2	3	_____
7. Organization	1	2	3	_____
8. Content/completeness	1	2	3	_____
9. Length	1	2	3	_____
10. Contact information	1	2	3	_____
11. Objective	1	2	3	_____
12. Experience	1	2	3	_____
13. Skills	1	2	3	_____
14. Accomplishments	1	2	3	_____
15. Education	1	2	3	_____
16. Other information	1	2	3	_____

6

SAVVY PRODUCTION

Once you've completed your final draft, you need to deal with certain production issues that also relate to key re - sume distribution issues. By anticipating these distribution issues, you should be able to produce a savvy resume that will function well when you distribute it to potential employers. Your goal should be to produce a first-class resume that projects your best professional image. It should nonverbally speak well of your style and attention to detail.

Distribution Affects Production

Let's assume, for the sake of organization, that you will be distributing your savvy resume via hand, mail, fax, and email. Each of these distribution methods has production implications. If, for example, you know you will be distributing your resume by hand or mail, then you need to deal with issues such as the quality and color of the paper. If you are requested to fax your resume, which is frequently the case with many employers today, paper color, type style, and font size become important issues, especially since colored papers and unconventional type styles and font sizes may not fax well. If you email your resume, you must deal with a whole new set of pro- duction issues, including format, layout, spacing, emphasizing techniques, characters per line, typefaces, word wrap, hyphenation, choice of word processing programs, files, and attachments. An emailed resume faces a whole new set of production issues that are often neglected by resume writers who assume they can just email the same resume they normally hand deliver, mail, or fax.

Relating to all of these distribution methods is the additional issue of scannability. Is your hand delivered, mailed, faxed, or emailed resume likely to be scanned into a resume database? If so, it should be both written and produced in a certain way so that it is compatible with today's scanning technology and screening approaches which emphasize the importance of keywords.

Ask Yourself

☑ Will your resume be scanned?

☑ What type styles and fonts work best?

☑ Should you include a photo on your resume?

☑ How long should your resume be?

☑ What paper weight and color works best?

Hand Delivered and Mailed Resumes

You may find many occasions when you will hand deliver your resume, especially as you network for information, advice, and referral, as well as mail it in response to a classified ad, prospect for job leads, or send it in response to a request for information on your qualifications. In fact, over 80 percent of all resumes are either mailed or hand delivered; many are simultaneously faxed, mailed, and emailed. In all of these situations, your resume should both look and feel good to the human eye and touch. Therefore, you need to address several of these "dress for success" production questions and issues:

■ How should you best design your resume?

- What type style and font should you use?

- When, what, and how should you highlight points?

- What type of paper (quality and color) should you use?

- What programs and equipment should you use?

- How should you print your resume?

- How should you produce or attach a two-page resume?

Let's address each of these issues and questions in the form of a handy checklist of resume production "rules":

❑ **Layout:** Your resume should be visually inviting to read. Remember, most readers only scan resumes. The more attractive the layout, the higher the probably the reader will invest more time in actually reading your resume. Failure to address key layout issues often means the content of a resume gets overlooked; it's simply not inviting to the reader because it looks unprofessional. If the layout is visually pleasing—like a first-class ad which nicely uses white space and eye-catching elements—you will attract the attention of your reader. Many attractive resumes use a two-column format—place the headings to the left and the descriptive material to the right. Other resumes center the headings followed by the descriptive material. In either case, single space within each section but double-space between sections. Avoid a cramped and crowded look that often appears in cases where the resume writer tries to get as much information crammed into a one or two-page resume as possible. Leave at least a 3/4" margin left to right and top to bottom. Always go for a quality look rather than a quantity look. Experiment with several alternative layouts until you achieve the right visual effect that is very pleasing to the eye. Look at examples of other resumes by asking yourself this question: Is this a visually-friendly resume that is very inviting to read and sustains my attention for more than ten seconds? If it's not, it needs to be laid out better. If layout is a not one of your strengths, see a graphic artist who may be able to suggest a very appealing design. But avoid too "artsy" of a look, which may include unnecessary graphic elements, that can turn off many readers. The focus should be on getting the reader to focus on the language and content of your resume—not be distracted by unique elements.

❏ **Type styles and font size:** Use a standard type style and proportionate font size, such as Times, Times Roman, Bookman, Palatino, and Garamond or a similar look-alike. Helvetica is a little harder to read but often gives a clean and modern look. Courier looks less professional—gives a decided "typewriter look" and is not a proportional font (spacing between letters is often awkward and thus distractive to readers who are used to proportionate spacing between letters). When in doubt, you're usually safe with Times Roman. Also, avoid very small or very large font sizes—below a 10-point or above a 12-point. An 11-point Times Roman with line spacing between 0.9 and 1.0 (or equivalent, depending on your word processing or desktop publishing program) usually works well.

❏ **Paper quality and color:** Your choice of paper quality and color says a lot about your professional style. The guiding principle here is to be both professional and conservative. This is not the place to make a special statement about your unconventional style. Remember, you want your reader to focus on the content, rather than the weight, texture, and color, of your resume. Such elements do count, but they should not be over-emphasized to the detriment of your resume content. You're usually best off choosing a good quality paper stock, between 20 and 50 lb. bond paper with 100 percent cotton fiber ("rag content") which may or may not include a watermark. This paper is readily available, and reasonably priced, in office supply stores as well as with most quick-copy printers. Avoid heavy textured papers that could feel oppressive and which may be difficult to scan. As for paper color, a bright or off-white paper is fine. It also will scan well. Avoid bright colored papers unless you are applying for a position that may encourage unconventional approaches, such as in art or advertising. Many executive candidates report success with a combination white and gray paper—a gray paper framed with a half-inch white border. This type of paper can be found in some office supply/stationery stores.

> You want your reader to focus on the content, rather than the weight, texture, and color, of your resume. Many candidates report success with a combination white and gray paper—a gray paper framed with a half-inch border.

❑ **Graphic elements and photos:** You should generally avoid embellishing a resume with graphic elements and photos, although there may be exceptions, depending on your audience. Photos, for example, are double-edged swords: you, your mother, or spouse may love your picture, but 50 percent of your audience may dislike it. The old adage that a *"picture is worth a thousand words"* may mean 500 of those words will be negative. Like advertising, you'll never know which 50 percent works in your favor! Graphic elements and photos follow the old rule of *"when in doubt, throw it out!"* Also, keep in mind that your resume may be scanned. Graphic elements and photos may disrupt other elements on a scanned resume. Keep your physical appearance a secret until you show up at the job interview.

❑ **Programs and equipment:** Most standard word processing programs and canned resume production programs will enable you to create a very professional-looking resume. However, a good desktop publishing program, such a PageMaker, QuarkXpress, or Ventura, will be even better. Always produce your resume on a computer that will enable you to save and change elements. Typewritten resumes say a lot about your current level of technology, or lack thereof. If you have a professional word processor or desktop publisher produce your resume, including developing an attractive layout and printing multiple copies, expect to pay between $50 and $100 for this work. Always use the best production equipment you can afford.

❑ **Printing options:** You achieve the best quality production with a laser printer and a high quality copy machine. Avoid dot matrix printers, which communicate a real amateur and mass production look. Again, put your best foot forward by using the best you can afford. In the case of printing options, the costs of going first-class are inexpensive. If you have a two-page resume, be sure each page is printed separately. Do not print a double-sided resume. Not only do they look cramped, they do not scan.

❑ **Collating:** Never staple a multi-page resume. Paper clips also are unnecessary. You should identify continuation pages a page notation at the top left side—Page 2. Remember, your resume may be scanned, and scanners don't like staples. It's also irritating to have to remove staples in order to make copies of your resume for other reviewers.

Faxed Resumes

When requested to fax your resume, you should fax the same copy that you would normally hand deliver or mail. This copy should be printed on white paper with black ink, preferably in a 11- or 12-point font size, for ease of readability at the other end. Resumes and letters using small fonts are often unreadable when faxed. Again, no photos or graphic elements, including shaded boxes, which do not fax well. Also, make sure your fax machine is working well—clean and with no lines running through the faxed pages. If you don't have a fax machine, many quick-copy and office supply places, such as Kinko's, Staples, and Office Depot, will send faxes for about $1.00 per page. Avoid computer-generated faxes since they tend to look like email, which raises another set of production issues altogether.

Scanned Resumes

Not all resumes are initially read by human beings. Indeed, many large companies and many government offices automatically use Optical Character Recognition (OCR) software to scan all resumes they receive. These programs enable HR departments to quickly store hundreds, indeed thousands, of resumes in databases as well as sort and retrieve them by keywords. If you know your resume is likely to be scanned (call an employer to find out if you're uncertain of their intake, retrieval, and screening/review processes), be sure your resume conforms to these 15 basic rules for writing and producing a scannable resume:

1. Print your resume on standard 8½" x 11" paper.

2. Produce the resume on 20 lb. white paper with black ink.

3. Use a laser printer that produces crisp and clear print.

4. Put your name at the top of each page.

5. Include a standard address format, on a separate line, under your name at the top of the first page.

6. Use a simple design—no photos or graphic elements such as boxes, reverses, or shading.

7. Avoid columns, vertical or horizontal lines, and abbreviations, other than common ones such as BA, MA, or Ph.D.

8. Select a standard type style, such as Times Roman or Courier, with sufficient space between letters; make sure the letters do not touch which sometimes happens with tight proportional fonts.

9. Keep the point size between 10 and 12 points.

10. Avoid using common emphasizing techniques such as underlining and italics.

11. Include numerous keywords—rich nouns rather than verbs—that emphasize your major skills and accomplishments.

12. Left justify only.

13. Maintain at least a 3/4" margin around the resume.

14. Do not fold or staple the resume.

15. Double-check for any possible spelling, grammatical, or punctuation errors.

Emailed Resumes

Email resumes follow a different set of writing and production rules. Sometimes referred to as "Internet resumes" or "plain text resumes," this type of resume is usually produced in a word processing document, saved as an ASCII or text only file, and then transmitted as email via the Internet. Depending on how the recipient handles such a resume, an emailed resume also may be entered into a resume database. Emailed resumes should follow these 13 basic rules:

1. Create an email version of your resume in your standard word processing program.

2. Set the left margin at 0 and the right margin at 65; each line must not exceed 65 characters.

3. Turn off word wrap or automatic hyphen; use a hard right return (hit "Enter" key) at the end of each line.

4. Select a fixed-width rather than proportional typeface. Your safest typeface choice is Courier.

5. Include a keyword summary, just in case this resume gets scanned into a resume database (that retrieves resumes by keywords).

6. Limit emphasizing techniques to these four: all caps, asterisks (*), dashes (-), and plus signs (+). Put your name and headings in ALL CAPS.

7. Use the Space bar and Enter key to create white space. Do not use the Tab key or other formatting commands to indent or center items.

8. Spell check the document.

9. Save your resume as a text only document, which converts it to a plain text, resume (ASCII document).

10. Check for formatting problems by reopening the document; fix any formatting problems using your Space bar and Enter key.

11. Drop the plain text resume into the body of your email message—do not send it as an attachment.

12. Before your email your resume to an employer, email it to yourself or a friend to check for any formatting problems.

13. When preparing to transmit your email resume to an employer, be sure to include an attention-getting yet professional subject line, such as "Information You Requested" or "Resume For Accounting Position."

While emailed resumes are relatively unadorned, this does not mean they have to be ugly ducklings. If you observe these basic rules, your emailed resume will look much better than most such resumes received by employers.

Always Present Your Best Self

Whatever you do, make sure the quality of your resume production at least equals the quality of your resume content. Remember, at every stage of the resume process, you are presenting your very best professional image. Most of the production issues identified here are important for projecting a professional image. While making writing errors can be deadly, making production errors can be just as deadly. Make sure your resume is not "dead upon arrival" because of production problems.

7

SAVVY DISTRIBUTION

Once you've created the perfect savvy resume, you need to turn your attention to key distribution issues. For the in the end, your resume is only as good as your distribution methods. Who, for example, should receive your resume? How will you send it—hand deliver or via mail, fax, or email? When should you fax or email a resume versus hand deliver or mail it? Will a next day delivery service enhance the visibility of your resume? Are employers more responsive to emailed and faxed resumes than those that arrive by snail mail? Should you primarily target your resume toward a few select employers or broadcast it to hundreds of potential employers? Is it a good idea to send a video resume or direct an employer to your homepage to see the full range of your talents?

These questions focus on key distribution issues that can make a big difference in whether or not your resume gets read and responded to with an invitation to a job interview. Neglect this issue and you may effectively sabotage what is otherwise an outstanding resume. If you distribute your savvy resume properly, you increase your chances of interviewing for the perfect job.

Distribution Options

Most job seekers fail to seriously address the issue of resume and letter distribution, which is so critical in determining their overall job search effectiveness. Introverted job seekers tend to select the most passive forms of distribution—mailing resumes to strangers with a generic "To Whom It May Concern" cover letter. Most extroverted job seekers understand the importance of conducting a proactive job search that includes a great deal of networking involving informational or referral interviewing. These job seekers literally hand deliver their resume to numerous individuals as well as mail, fax, and email their resumes to many potential employers. If you tend to be a relatively introverted individual—reluctant to approach strangers about your employment interests and needs— you should seriously consider how you can best approach the many distribution issues raised in this chapter. Your effectiveness will be determined by how well you distribute your savvy resume

Ask Yourself

☑ How will I distribute my resume?

☑ Is it best to mail, fax, or email a resume?

☑ Are resume videos and homepages effective?

☑ What distribution errors should I avoid?

☑ Is it a good idea to broadcast my resume to hundreds of employers?

☑ Should I send my resume by FedEx?

in the process of communicating your qualifications to employers. Distribution options begin with one major strategic question: Should you primarily target your resume toward specific employers you know are interested in your qualifications or should you broadcast it to numerous employers who by chance might be interested in you? Once you've addressed this question, many of the other distribution issues fall in place.

Targeting Versus Broadcasting

It's always tempting to cast a large net by broadcasting your resume to hundreds of potential employers. After all, as the logic goes, someone out there must be interested in your qualifications—if only you could get them to read your resume. Why not send out as much paper as possible in the hope of finding such a person? Unfortunately, there is little evidence that such an approach is very effective. Some people indeed do get job leads this way that eventually result in job interviews and offers. The problem is that this method is similar to the art of direct-mail— under the best of circumstances, which means using a very good mailing list of anxious prospects, don't expect more than a 1 percent response rate. This means that for every 1,000 resumes you send out, you may get 10 employers who contact you for more information and perhaps invitations to job interviews. If you up the numbers, say to 10,000 resumes, you can expect to get proportionately more "hits." Not many novice job seekers can afford spending hundreds, indeed thousands, of dollars sustaining such a direct-mail campaign.

Broadcasting is the method of choice for many introverts and individuals who want to feel like they are doing something to further their job search without having to invest their ego too much in the process. It puts them in motion—they feel they are at least doing something about their job search, however ineffective. Indeed, broadcasting often gives one a false sense of making progress. You put your resume in the mail and then wait for the phone to ring or you check your email messages for employer responses. This can all be done in the comfort of your home by using a computer and by making one big trip to the mailbox or Post Office. You don't have to engage in any of those more extroverted job search activities we outlined at the end of Chapter 4, especially picking up the telephone to expand networking contacts, speaking with potential employers, or writing to specific individuals about job opportunities.

The best way to broadcast your resume is to get it in as many resume databases as possible. You can easily go online and enter your resume into the resume databases of hundreds of employment sites on the Internet. Start with these top sites and keep moving on to other appealing sites:

www.monster.com	*www.nationjob.com*
www.careerpath.com	*www.hotjobs.com*
www.careermosiac.com	*www.net-temps.com*
www.jobsearch.org	*www.dice.com*
www.headhunter.net	*www.careerbuilder.com*

Other broadcast approaches that might prove useful would be focused on specific employers and headhunters you know are *in a hiring mode* in your particular area of expertise. In this case, the quality of your mailing list is critical. If, for example, you have fifteen years of progressive experience in pharmaceutical sales, you may want to broadcast your resume and cover letter only to those headhunters who specialize in pharmaceutical sales and those pharmaceutical companies that are looking for experienced salespeople. Do not just broadcast your resume to any company with a sales force. The key to increasing the probability of getting responses from your mailing is to target your broadcast approach by using a highly specialized mailing list which you either develop on your own—based upon your knowledge of your industry—or rent from a list broker or a resume broadcast firm. But to simply send out your resume to hundreds of anonymous and undifferentiated employers is probably a big waste of time and money.

Hand Delivery

The best way to deliver a resume is by hand—your hand. It means you've moved your resume closer to a job interview than if you had sent it by mail, fax, or email. This does not mean you should travel to an employer's office and hand deliver your resume; that would be presumptuous, odd, too assertive, and probably brand you as "too hungry" for the job. Rather, it means you are engaged in an active networking campaign whereby you use your resume to get information, advice, and referrals. Near the end of the referral interview, you ask the person to examine your resume (1) for feedback on the appropriateness of your resume to the type of position you discussed; (2) to get advice on how to strengthen your resume; and (3) to be remembered for future reference. You then follow-up this meeting with a nice thank-you letter accompanied by a copy of your revised resume for the individual's reference and any future referrals. For more information on this distribution method, see our book on networking for job seekers: *Dynamite Networking For Dynamite Jobs.*

Snail Mail

Despite the rise of the digital age that calls this method "snail mail," because it's not super fast, most resumes still travel by mail. It's still one of the most effective distribution methods, especially since it enables you to showcase several aspects of your professionalism. For many employers, there is still nothing like a nice crisp, well-crafted, and attention-grabbing letter and resume arriving in the mail. In fact, many people will open and respond to their mail at a much higher rate than to email, which is often cluttered with noise.

> **Many people will open and respond to their mail at a much higher rate than to email, which is often cluttered with noise.**

You can easily speed up the delivery of snail mail by spending $15 to $20 on using the next-day delivery methods of FedEx, UPS, or Airborne or by spending $3.20 on two-day Priority Mail delivered via the U.S. Postal Service. While these speedy delivery methods also may momentarily (five seconds) grab the attention of the recipient by indicating the enclosed material is probably urgent, on the other hand, the likely recipient is often someone in the mailroom or someone authorized to screen mail. When in doubt as to the effectiveness of speedy delivery methods, go with the U.S. Post Office's $3.20 two-day Priority Mail which probably impresses the mail room and screener as much as the more expensive next-day delivery methods.

If you are quickly responding to a classified ad by using speedy delivery methods, the assumption that *"the early bird gets the worm"* may not be true. Since 80 percent of the responses to an ad usually arrive within a week, the last letter and resume to arrive may get more attention simply because it's not surrounded by so many other distracting "early birds."

Fax

Many employers request that you send them a copy of your letter and resume by fax. Doing so is both fast and convenient. It's especially efficient for recipients who do not constantly check their email.

It's best to fax a copy of your original resume, which should be designed to be mailed, rather than generate a faxed copy from your computer fax program. An original maintains key layout and formatting elements that communicate your unique professional image.

Do not send a resume as a junk fax. Treat fax numbers as "by invitation only." Since many people get irritated with unsolicited faxes, your resume will be "dead upon arrival" if sent without prior notice or without an invitation to do so.

A faxed resume should always be accompanied by a cover letter, which is addressed to a specific person. If you don't have the person's name, call for the information or leave out the salutation altogether. Avoid what may appear to be "cute" or "fun' cover sheets; they may appear "dumb" and "unprofessional" to our fax recipient!

Email

More and more employers prefer receiving resumes and letters by email. Not only is this distribution method efficient, it also separates the technical "haves" and "have nots." Relatively unadorned, email resumes tend to be very content-oriented: employers focus on the content of the resume rather than the many distractive "dress for success" design, layout, and graphic elements that often accompany mailed and faxed resumes. Such resumes also enable employers to quickly move resumes into electronic databases without having to handle paper. Therefore, it's important that you have an email version of your resume available at all times that adheres to our email resume rules in Chapter 6.

Many email users make the mistake of sending their resume as an attachment that requires the recipient to open a file. Unless requested to do otherwise, always include your resume in the body of your email message; it may not look pretty, but it's safe. Many people automatically discard attachments rather than take a chance on catching someone's virus. Sending a virus is another way to have your resume classified as "dead upon arrival."

Be very careful in how you use email in your job search. First, treat email as "by invitation only" communication channels. Do not assume, because you have someone's email address, that the recipient's email is an open mailbox for unsolicited messages. On the other hand, many companies welcome email resumes by actually soliciting them on their homepages and in classified ads in newspapers and on the Internet. They have specific email addresses reserved for resumes and letters. When in doubt as to the "openness" of an email address, call and ask if the individual prefers receiving your communication by email, fax, or mail. In many cases, even heavy email users will want you to channel your communication by fax or mail which gets their more immediate attention.

Second, be sure to *always* check your spelling and grammar before sending email. In other words, like all written job search communication, your email messages should be perfect. If not, they will communicate negative messages about your level of literacy and professionalism; at best you will appear careless and seem not to take this employer seriously enough to warrant your best professional effort.

Videos and Homepages

Be very cautious in your decision to include multimedia elements in your job search. If you choose to create a video resume and/or recommend that employers link to your homepage, your productions must be top quality. If not, you will create a negative impression that could kill your candidacy. As soon as you introduce video and multimedia elements, you shift your job search to a different level that raises new and controversial issues. Like putting a photo on your resume, you may like it, but others may or may not. The problem is you don't know which recipients will dislike you.

However, a video resume or homepage can enhance your job search, if you are in a field that needs to showcase specific talents related to the video and homepage—modeling, theater, entertainment, graphic art, and Web design skills. But your effort must be first-class. Many amateurs include inappropriate information or project an unprofessional image through these highly visual mediums. Be very careful when you consider going down these two roads. They involve many important communication issues.

Distribution Errors to Avoid

Many job seekers make a variety of distribution errors that ensure their resume never sees the light of day. The most common such errors you should avoid are these:

1. Sent to the wrong person or department.

2. Addressed to an anonymous and suggestive "To Whom It May Concern," "Dear Sir," "Dear Madam," or "Dear Future Employer."

3. Addresses the employer by his or her first name: "Dear Tom" in a letter and "Hi Tom" in email.

4. Arrives without a cover letter or with just a business card attached or with a presumptuous note scribbled at the top of the resume (*"Hi, here's my resume. Hope to meet with you soon!"* Mary).

5. Includes a poorly written cover letter filled with spelling and grammatical errors.

6. Includes an unnecessary and boring cover letter that merely repeats what's on the resume.

7. Includes a weird, cutsy, or other type of unconventional cover letter that brings into question the individual's motivations, abilities, professionalism, and mental state.

8. Folded numerous times and inserted in a very small envelope—will never lay flat or may be put at the bottom of the weighty pile to improve its flatness!

9. Double-sealed with tape to be certain it won't fall out of the envelope—a real struggle for the recipient to open who probably rightly concludes this individual is most likely compulsive.

10. Arrives in a big box in the hopes of really grabbing the employer's attention (but this sometimes works in the case of certain sales positions).

11. Delivered by mail without the proper postage attached —makes a really negative impression when the recipient gets to pay "postage due."

12. Includes several unsolicited enclosures, such as transcripts, samples of work, and self-serving letters of recommendation, that distract from the central message of the cover letter and resume.

13. Arrives after the application deadline or after the position has been filled.

14. Includes a hastily handwritten note on the back of the envelope.

15. Re-sends the same mailed, faxed, or emailed resume every few days to really get the person's attention—and irritation as a real pest.

Do What's Really Important

Savvy resume distributors keep an eye on what is really important to their job search. Like their focused savvy resume, they remain employer-oriented. In attempting to find a job that is a perfect "fit" for both them and the employer, they target specific employers who need their skills. They don't waste time and money on broadcasting their resume to hundreds of employers. They know how to best connect with the right employers. Luck comes their way because they have worked hard in developing a highly proactive resume distribution, and job search, campaign.

8

Savvy Follow-Up

So what do you plan to do after you've distributed your resume? Will you take certain actions or wait to be called by an employer? If you wait, chances are you may never hear and you'll waste time speculating about a particular job. If you take action, you can move on to the job interview or on to other more promising job leads.

Waiters and Initiators

Waiting is not a good job search strategy. If you want action, you must take action. Indeed, the longer your wait, the higher the probability you will never hear from an employer. If you concluded your cover letter with the standard hopeful *"I look forward to hearing from you"* closing, there's a good probability the employer may not contact you. It's best to start with the assumption that there is a high probability the employer will not respond to your written communication, regardless of whether it is mailed, faxed, or emailed. Therefore, you must take more action to get the employer to respond to you in positive ways.

Consider, on the other hand, what might happen if you concluded your letter with one of these three follow-up statements:

I'll call you Thursday afternoon to answer any questions you may have concerning how I can best meet your needs.

or

I'll call you Thursday afternoon to answer any questions you may have concerning my candidacy.

or

I'll call you Thursday afternoon to see if we can arrange a mutually convenient time to meet for an interview.

These follow-up statements move you from a passive resume distributor, who waits for others to take action, to a *proactive* candidate, who seeks action through one of the most effective channels of communication—the telephone. You must become proactive in today's job market. Hiring realities are such that employers are very busy people. Many of them spend only a few seconds reading resumes and letters. If you want

Ask Yourself

☑ What's the best way to follow-up?

☑ What do I do if I get voicemail?

☑ How can I best overcome resistance?

☑ How should I handle gatekeepers?

☑ What should I say when I call?

them to take you more seriously, forewarn them that you will be making a follow-up call. This often results in the recipient spending a little more time reading your resume and letter. He or she also may view you as a more serious candidate who exhibits a positive behavioral trait—you take initiative in following-up on business.

Timing

When is the best time to follow-up your resume and letter? You should state in your cover letter that you will make a follow-up call within three working days after you can expect the employer to receive your correspondence. If you emailed or faxed your resume and letter, make the follow-up call within three days. If you mailed your resume and letter, depending on how far the mail must travel, you'll probably want to make the call within seven days. If you wait longer, chances are the recipient may not remember receiving your correspondence or your resume and letter will not be fresh in his memory. There's a good chance that your anticipated phone call will move your resume to the top of the pile, which is where you want to be as the employer gets closer to making final screening decisions.

Overcoming Resistance

Not all employers want candidates to make follow-up calls. Indeed, many of them state in their ads *"No phone calls."* Honor that request but don't give up on taking follow-up action. At least try to follow-up by email, fax, or mail.

If you say you will call, be sure you actually make the call. Failure to follow-through says something important about your behavior— you may have a short attention span or maybe you're unreliable.

If you call at your stated time and encounter voice mail or a gatekeeper, do the following:

▶ **Voice mail:** Leave a nice message saying you called and mentioning that you will call back again:

> *Hi, this is Jeff Martin. I'm calling in reference to my letter and resume of March 7 in which I mentioned I would call*

you today. My phone number is 328-3721. If I don't hear
from you later today, I'll give you a call tomorrow morning
around 10:30. I look forward to speaking with you.

Leave your phone number, but do not expect the person
to return your phone call. By stating you will call back at
a particular time, you put the individual on notice that
you will not go away by just hoping to hear from them
with a return call. Keep leaving the same message in sub-
sequent calls. However, if you
don't make personal contact after
eight calls, give up and move on
to someone who is more responsive. At this point, you are close
to making yourself a pleasant-na-
tured pest, someone the employer
really doesn't want to talk with.
However, many employers will return your call after you leave five

> Many employers re-
> turn your call after
> five messages. If you
> don't make personal
> contact after eight
> calls, give up and
> move on to some-
> one who is more re-
> sponsive.

messages. Some feel a sense of guilt for not returning your
call or they just want you to go away. In either case, you'll
make contact so you can move on to other more productive job search activities. Your goal here is bring closure—
either positive or negative—to this particular job lead.
Under no circumstances should you indicate irritation at
not having your phone calls returned. Remember, your
assumption should be that your call will not be returned,
at least not the first five calls.

▶ **Gatekeepers:** If you call and get a real person, such as a
receptionist or assistant, use a similar telephone script:

Hi, this is Jeff Martin calling for Ms. Ketterling. Is she available?

If you're told she is not available and if you would like to leave a message, ask when she might be free and then leave a similar I'll-call-her-again message:

Yes, could you tell her Jeff Martin called? I'm calling in reference to my letter of March 7. My number is 328-3721. If I don't hear from her later today, I'll give her a call again tomorrow morning around 10:30. Thank you.

Make a few of these follow-up calls, and you may make friends with the gatekeeper. After awhile he or she may put in a good word for you—that nice person who keeps calling—and persuade your letter recipient to either accept or return your call.

Being Competent and Likable

Behind every savvy resume should be a savvy job seeker whose job search behavior complements his work behavior. You want to be savvy at each stage of your job search, from writing resumes and letters to networking, following-up job leads, interviewing for the job, and negotiating the terms of employment. At each stage, you and your behavior are on display. Regardless of how well qualified you appear on paper, your behavior during the job search says a great deal about how well you may work with the employer both professionally and personally. Therefore, you need to project an image of both competence and likability—you're someone the employer will enjoy working with because you "fit in" with the organization. If you do this, you should be well on your way to getting a dream job you both do well and enjoy doing.

9

SAVVY RESUME SAMPLER

The savvy resume principles outlined in previous chapters are illustrated here in a few carefully selected examples of be-havior-based resumes. Our first example, Jason Davis on pages 128–133, sets the framework for developing a savvy resume. Here, we include two examples of his resume—before (traditional) and after (savvy). The first example on pages 128–129 is his original resume, which he developed in reference to the standard resume writing advice found in most resume writing books as well as pro-vided by some traditional career advisors. For many people, includ-ing employers, this appears to be a good resume. However, in closer examination—and based upon the issues and principles we discussed earlier—this is a traditional chronological resume with many of the problems associated with this choice of format. As such, it has these two characteristics which actually become major weaknesses for this type of resume:

- **Lacks a central organizing Objective for focusing each element in the resume**. Since it's unclear what Jason wants to do for an employer, the employer must analyze and interpret the resume in reference to his own needs. Thus, Jason fails to target the needs of the employer and set the agenda for discussing his candidacy in a job inter-view.

- **Organizes his Professional Experience as his chronology of work history**. Focuses on outlining the formal duties and responsibilities normally assigned to positions. Reveals nothing about actual accomplishments—results, outcomes, or benefits the employer received when he performed various duties and responsibilities. The reader of this resume only learns that Jason Davis *held positions* that involved certain types of work. He learns nothing about accomplishments or a desirable pattern of behavior. At best, the employer must interpret or speculate what might be this person's accomplishments and motivated pattern of behavior.

The second example significantly transforms Jason's traditional chronological resume into a behavior-based resume. Notice the dramatic change in focus. This resume has the following strengths as outlined in previous chapters:

- Includes a well-defined Objective that incorporates both *skills* and *outcomes* relevant to the employer.

- Develops a strong Qualification Summary that outlines the basic elements in Jason's motivated pattern of behavior as well as includes keywords that should perform well if this resume is scanned.

- Showcases major accomplishments in the form of employer-oriented *results, outcomes, or benefits*. These accomplishments are the basic building blocks of Jason's motivated behavioral pattern—he tells the reader what he has accomplished in the past so that the reader can infer that these consistent accomplishments will continue in the future. His accomplishments fit into two types of highly sought-after, and hopefully predictable, bottom line benefits—saves money and generates additional income for the employer.

- Incorporates numerous "keywords" throughout the resume, especially in the Qualification Summary and Computer Skills sections. A highly scannable resume.

The remaining examples repeat these principles that are the basis for writing employer-oriented of behavior-based resume. The emphasis is always on goals and outcomes that will communicate a motivated pattern of behavior to employers. Our final example, the classic "T" letter, actually substitutes for a regular resume. It incorporates the basic elements of a behavior-based resume but does so in the form of a letter. This is one of the most powerful job search letters, which tends to generate many positive responses from employers. For more information on how to write such letters, see *Haldane's Best Cover Letters For Professionals* (Impact, 2000).

JASON DAVIS

2417 North Wells
Orlando, FL 33333
Tel. 321-123-4567
Email: jdavis@netme.com

SUMMARY

Detailed oriented individual with strong analytical skills in accounting and financial systems. Adept at using statistical and other forecasting models for developing budgets. Proven ability to create and implement cost management systems using ABC models. Proficient in using relevant software programs, such as Deltek, MAS90, Peachtree, Excel, Quicken, Microsoft Office, Turbo-Tax, WordPerfect, Corel, and ABC Flowchart.

EDUCATION

University of Illinois	MBA, Finance	1997
Vanderbilt University	BA, Accounting	1991

PROFESSIONAL EXPERIENCE

DELTA COMPUTER SERVICES, Orlando, FL   Controller   1996–Present

- Responsible for developing operational, cash, and capital budgets. Coordinate with all divisions of the company in all facets of the budgeting process. Provide support for budget variance analysis.

- Analyze financial statements and other related reports, using ratio analysis, to identify possible weaknesses in the company's financial operations and structure and recommend remedial actions.

- Coordinate the treasury function that includes cash management, investment strategies, and maintaining positive relationships with banks and investors.

- Prepare and submit Incurred Cost Submission on multi-million dollar government contracts.

- Monitor the company's accounting system to assure proper cost accumulation and that the system is in compliance with AACD regulations.

THE TRAINING GROUP, Atlanta, GA   Senior Accountant   1991–1995

- Managed a staff of two junior Accountants

- Responsible for all facets of accounting: accounts payable, receivable, payroll functions, general ledger account reconciliation and bank reconciliation.

- Prepared Corporate Financial Statements including Income Statements, Balance Sheets Cash Flow Statements for both internal and external reporting requirements.

- Prepared and filed all corporate tax returns including payroll related taxes, sales, property, and other State and Federal taxes.

- Used cost-volume profit and differential cost analysis to aid management in evaluating new project development and setting performance targets.

- Developed sensitivity models for determining break-even sales volume for each corporate division.

CONSULTING SERVICES. Provides accounting and financial services on a consulting basis to various small and medium-sized companies, such as:

West Gate Products	Orlando, FL	1997–present
eOffice Supplies	Orlando, FL	1998–present
Abrams Technologies	Jacksonville, FL	1995–1998
Great Georgia Fabrics	Atlanta, GA	1991–1993

PROFESSIONAL AFFILIATION

Member of American Association of Individual Investors, American Society of Accounts, and Society of Investment Analysts

JASON DAVIS

2417 North Wells
Orlando, FL 33333
Tel. 321-123-4567
Email: jdavis@netme.com

OBJECTIVE

A challenging position using skills in **Financial Analysis, Security Analysis, Budget Analysis**, and **Investment Strategies** that will be used to:

- strengthen a company's financial position

- identify new investment opportunities

- develop effective financial strategies

- forecast and manage future performance

QUALIFICATION SUMMARY

Detailed and results-oriented individual with strong analytical and entrepreneurial skills in accounting and financial systems. Adept at using statistical and other forecasting models for creating budgets, improving business operations, and developing investment strategies. Proven ability to create and implement effective cost management systems. Over 8 years of progressive responsibility and expertise in financial environments dealing with:

ACCOMPLISHMENTS

Financial Analysis/Planning	Investment Analysis	Accounting
Strategic Planning	Cash Management	Contracting
Credit Analysis	Budget Analysis	Valuation
Mergers and Acquisitions	Financial Management	Research
E-commerce	Risk Management	Project Management

FINANCE

- Managed financial operation of government contractor with $15 million in assets and $25 million in annual revenue. **Results:** Saved over $50,000 in annual accounting costs by strengthening leadership over all accounting, payroll, banking, and risk management functions.

- Analyzed financial statements and other related reports, using ratio analysis to identify possible weaknesses in the company's financial operations and recommended remedial actions. **Results:** Improved procedures enabled company to develop aggressive marketing strategy for generating an addition $5 million in revenue.

- Developed and administered new defined contribution, profit sharing, and cafeteria plans. **Results:** Employee turnover reduced by 20 percent over a 12-month period.

- Prepared reports that summarized and forecasted company business activity based on past, present, and expected operations. Used various forecasting techniques, such as regression, moving averages, and other econometic models, to establish the forecasted figures. **Results:** Earnings forecasts, which were 95 percent accurate in the first six months, established new investment strategy for achieving a 20 percent annual growth rate.

- Created the operational, cash, and capital budgets of several small companies. Introduced simplified small business accounting software programs to manage day-to-day accounting functions. **Results:** Saved each business over $30,000 annually by eliminating the need for a full-time accountant.

- Developed several proposals for clients doing business in the government-contracting industry. **Results:** Proposals responded to over $200 million in RFPs of which $125 million was awarded.

ACCOUNTING

- Defended employer before Contract Board of Appeals. **Results:** Saved employer over $200,000 in disallowed contract costs emanating from a FTAC audit.

- Performed all facets of accounting, including accounts payable, receivable, payroll functions, and general ledger account reconciliation and bank reconciliation statements. **Results:** Eliminated the need for two part-time bookkeeping positions and thus saved employer over $40,000 a year in personnel costs.

- Prepared corporate financial statements, including income statements, balance sheets, and cash flow statements for both internal and external reporting. **Results:** Improved on-time reporting by 300% within first six months and developed attractive financial portfolio for generating $8 million in outside investment.

- Introduced a budgetary system that inculcated a culture of cost control awareness. **Results:** Streamlined the service delivery system of a training company and saved over $100,000 annually in wasteful processes.

- Developed sensitivity models for determining break-even sales volume for each corporate division. **Results:** Improved profitability of five divisions by 15 percent within six months and eliminated one unprofitable division which saved the company more than $200,000.

- Prepared cost-volume profit and differential cost analysis to aid management in evaluating new project development and setting performance targets. **Results:** Reduced project evaluation time by over 60 percent and consistently met new performance targets in record time.

PROFESSIONAL EXPERIENCE

DELTA COMPUTER SERVICES, Orlando, FL   1996–Present
Controller

THE TRAINING GROUP, Atlanta, GA   1991–1995
Senior Accountant

SEVEN SMALL BUSINESSES   1989–Present
Part-time consultant in various aspects of accounting

EDUCATION

University of Illinois   MBA, Finance   1997

- Developed award-winning e-commerce business model for teaching undergraduate students

- Interned with Arthur Andersen as Investment Analyst

Vanderbilt University   BA, Accounting   1991

- Graduated with Honors, 3.8/4.0

- Worked full-time in earning 100% of educational and personal expenses

COMPUTER SKILLS

- Microsoft Word   ■ Excel   ■ Access   ■ Windows   ■ PowerPoint
- PageMaker   ■ PhotoShop   ■ Lotus Notes

MEMBERSHIPS & AFFILIATIONS

- Society of Investment Analysts   ■ American Society of Accountants
- American Association of Individual Investors   ■ Toastmasters International

James Nelson

Email: jnelson@walt.com

553 Wedgewood Court   Indianapolis, IN 44444   321-321-3210

Objective

A management position with an aggressive start-up firm that recognizes the importance of combining proven skills in Project and Marketing Management to achieve remarkable growth opportunities.

Personal Profile

A no-nonsense self-starter who visualizes new possibilities and quickly makes things happen. A strong, analytical, and highly focused team leader who anticipates and systematically tackles issues before they become problems. A manager's manager who efficiently and effectively takes on complex challenges with energy and enthusiasm.

Qualifications

More than 10 years experience using key technical and interpersonal skills for achieving exceptional results:

- Project Management
- Goal Setting
- Problem Solving
- Supervision
- Evaluation
- Marketing and Sales
- Design and Innovate
- Team Building
- Conceptualize and Create
- Take Charge

Achievements

Project Management

- Developed innovative scheduling technique to track more than 800 activities affecting the construction of seven commercial buildings worth more than $50 million. **Results:** Shortened project completion time by four months and saved the company $135,000 in costs.

- Resolved construction delays on three major projects. **Results:** Avoided $80,000 in construction penalties and persuaded concerned clients to initiated $3 million in additional construction.

- Completed two-month, $300,000 project six days ahead of schedule. **Result:** Satisfied customer awarded company a new two-year, $25 million project with a built-in $200,000 incentive bonus to complete the project two months early. Project completed in timely fashion and awarded bonus.

Marketing Management

- Developed start-up firm specializing in commercial security systems. **Results:** Generated $3 million in revenues within two years and expanded profitability by 20% each year.

- Started a limited real estate partnership with $1,000 of seed money. **Results:** Grossed more than $1 million in revenue within the first six months of operation.

- Persuaded City Council members to develop new pedestrian mall and recreation area in downtown Evansville. **Results:** Publicity generated a 20% increase in clientele.

Experience

Jet-Way Construction Inc., Indianapolis, IN 1997–present
    Vice-President of Marketing/Operations

New Millennium Homes, Chicago, IL 1992–1996
    Sales Representative

QuestMar Associates, Gary, IN 1987–1991
    Construction Supervisor and Inspector

Education

University of Illinois, Campaign, IL 1987
    BS in Engineering

Additional Education and Training 1990–present
    Certificate in Architectural Design (Roosevelt University)
    Business Administration courses (Northeast University)
    Management training workshops (AMC Institute of Management)

Mary Taylor   Email: mtaylor@sky.com

184 Jefferson Highway   Philips, MA 02222   111-222-3333

Objective

A consulting position with a dynamic technology firm where proven skills in Management of Information Systems will be used for developing new and innovative e-commerce initiatives.

Professional Profile

A focused and decisive team leader who seeks intellectually challenging projects. Enjoy working with complex systems that require thorough analysis followed by cost-effective approaches. Always on time and usually under budget, no challenge is too great if analyzed from a unique perspective.

Qualifications

Over 7 years experience working with complex technical and managerial systems requiring the use of these key skills:

Technical	General
■ Windows 98	■ Analysis and solve problems
■ NT Server	■ Motivate and direct others
■ Oracle	■ Lead diverse design teams
■ Visual C++	■ Plan, organize, and coordinate
■ COBOL	■ Design and implement projects
■ Lotus Notes	■ Set and achieve difficult goals
■ Visual/Basic	■ Take charge
■ Novell NetWare	■ Accept responsibility

Selected Accomplishments

- Developed innovative e-commerce program for a leading coffee company. **Results:** Completed project 5% under budget, two weeks early, and with a design that has become a model for this industry.

- Created in-house training program to help customer administer own Website. **Result:** Reduced help desk calls by 25% and expanded e-commerce by 40% within six months.

- Designed the technology infrastructure for a start-up Internet Service Provider. **Results:** Completed project three weeks early and $5,000 under budget. Company currently enjoys $20 million in annual revenues and continues to use design services on a regular basis.

- Developed software interface that allowed non-secure computer to encrypt and transmit information to a secure host system. **Results:** Eliminated redundant systems which, in turn, saved company more than $2 million in operating costs.

- Planned the merger and relocation of two data processing facilities, one in Iowa and another in Oklahoma, into a single regional center in West Virginia. **Results:** Completed project five days early and 10% under budget. Relocation and merger now saves company more than $1 million a year.

- Created an innovative monthly billing system to process invoices for 10,000 clients. **Results:** Completed project 10 days early. New system saved company $7,000 a month by eliminating redundant procedures. Currently developing an online billing options that should save the company an additional $10,000 a month.

Experience

Web Solutions, Inc., Austin, TX   1997–present
Vice President, IT Officer

E-Biz Corporation, Houston, TX   1995–1997
Communication Specialist

United States Navy   1982–1994
Non-Commissioned Officer
    Webmaster for Naval Personnel Office in Washington, DC
    Responsible for Communications/Data Operations Center in Norfolk, VA
    In charge of Communications/Data Operations Center at San Diego, CA

Education and Training

Old Dominion University, Norfolk, VA
B.S., Computer Science

NCO Leadership School, San Diego, CA

Communications/Computer Systems Technical School, U.S. Navy, Norfolk, VA

January 23, 2000

Gerald Rostner
Silver Lake Products
873 Timberlake Drive
Phoenix, AZ 88888

Dear Mr. Rostner:

I'm responding to your job announcement that appeared on the CareerWeb site yesterday for a Public Relations Specialist. My resume is available online (#281481) with CareerWeb and I emailed a copy to you yesterday per your instructions.

I believe I may be the perfect candidate for this position given my more than eight years of progressive, results-oriented experience in Public Relations.

Your Requirements	**My Qualifications**
5+ years of experience in PR	8+ years of experience in PR as well as sales and marketing. I understand the important relationship between PR and sales and marketing.
Strong interpersonal skills.	Consistently praised on annual performance appraisal as *"adept in working well with both co-workers and clients."* Twice received "Employee of the Year" Award.
Ability to bring in new accounts.	Maintained and significantly expanded (20% annually) client base of key accounts that generate 30% of employer's total revenue base—up from 5% when hired three years ago.
Energetic and willing to travel.	Work well with deadlines and stressful situations. Energy and enthusiasm often cited by clients as a main reason for working with Joan Riley. Love to travel and do so frequently in working with clients and participating in professional activities.

In addition, I know the importance of building strong customer relations and developing innovative approaches to today's new PR mediums. I love taking on new challenges, working in multiple team and project settings, and seeing clients achieve results from my company's efforts.

I believe there is a strong match between your needs and my professional interests and qualifications. Could we meet soon to discuss how we might best work together? I'll call your office Thursday at 2pm to see if your schedule might permit such a meeting.

I appreciate your consideration and look forward to speaking with you Thursday afternoon.

Sincerely,

Joan Riley

Joan Riley

About the Authors

Ronald L. Krannich, Ph.D. and Caryl Rae Krannich, Ph.D., are two of America's leading business and travel writers who have authored more than 40 books. They currently operate Development Concepts Inc., a training, consulting, and publishing firm. A former Peace Corps Volunteer and Fulbright Scholar, Ron received his Ph.D. in Political Science from Northern Illinois University. Caryl received her Ph.D. in Speech Communication from Penn State University.

Ron and Caryl are former university professors, high school teachers, management trainers, and consultants. As trainers and consultants, they have completed numerous projects on management, career development, local government, population planning, and rural development in the United States and abroad.

The Krannichs' business and career work encompasses nearly 30 books they have authored on a variety of subjects: key job search skills, public speaking, government jobs, international careers, nonprofit organizations, and career transitions. Their work represents one of today's most extensive and highly praised collections of career and business writing: *101 Dynamite Answers to Interview Questions, 101 Secrets of Highly Effective Speakers, 201 Dynamite Job Search Letters, The Best Jobs For the 21st Century, Change Your Job Change Your Life, The Complete Guide to International Jobs and Careers, Discover the Best Jobs For You, Dynamite Cover Letters, Dynamite Resumes, Dynamite Salary Negotiations, Dynamite Tele-Search, The Educator's Guide to Alter-*

native Jobs and Careers, Find a Federal Job Fast, From Air Force Blue to Corporate Gray, From Army Green to Corporate Gray, From Navy Blue to Corporate Gray, Resumes and Job Search Letters For Transitioning Military Personnel, High Impact Resumes and Letters, International Jobs Directory, Interview For Success, Jobs and Careers With Nonprofit Organizations, Jobs For People Who Love Travel, and *Dynamite Networking For Dynamite Jobs.* Their books are found in most major bookstores, libraries, and career centers as well as on Impact's Web site: *www.impactpublications.com.* Many of their works are available interactively on CD-ROM (*The Ultimate Job Source*).

Ron and Caryl live a double career life. Authors of 13 travel books, the Krannichs continue to pursue their international interests through their innovative and highly acclaimed Impact Guides travel series (*"The Treasures and Pleasures…Best of the Best"*) which currently encompasses separate titles on Italy, France, China, Hong Kong, Thailand, Indonesia, Singapore, Malaysia, India, and Australia. When not found at their home and business in Virginia, they are probably somewhere in Europe, Asia, Africa, the Middle East, the South Pacific, or the Caribbean pursuing one of their major passions—researching and writing about quality arts and antiques.

The Krannichs reside in Northern Virginia. Frequent speakers and seminar leaders, they can be contacted through the publisher or by email: *krannich@impactpublications.com*

INDEX

video, 36, 117
writers, 10
Retention, 2, 48

S

Salary, 21
Savvy, 4-6
Screening, 6, 48-49
Skills, 8
Success Factor Analysis, 78-84
Supports, 7, 67

T

Telephone, 121
Testing, 48-49
Time:
   best, 122
   finding, 60-62
   passive, 60-62
   proactive, 60-62
Targeting, 111-113
Type style, 103

U

Unemployment, 2
Unique you, 51-52

V

Voice mail, 122-123

W

Work history, 13

BUSINESS AND CAREER RESOURCES

Contact Impact Publications for a free annotated listing of resources or visit the World Wide Web for a complete listing of resources: www.impactpublications.com. The following books are available directly from Impact Publications. Complete the following form or list the titles, include postage (see formula at the end), enclose payment, and send your order to:

IMPACT PUBLICATIONS
9104-N Manassas Drive
Manassas Park, VA   20111-5211
Tel 1-800/361-1055, 703/361-7300, or Fax 703/335-9486
Quick and easy online ordering: *www.impactpublications.com*

Qty.	Titles	Price	Total

BUSINESS ESSENTIALS

_____ 101 Mistakes Employers Make and How to Avoid Them	14.95	_____
_____ 101 Secrets of Highly Effective Speakers	14.95	_____
_____ The Best 100 Web Sites for HR Professionals	12.95	_____
_____ Employer's Guide to Recruiting on the Internet	24.95	_____
_____ Recruit and Retain the Best	14.95	_____
_____ Take This Job and Thrive	14.95	_____

RESUMES & LETTERS

_____ 100 Winning Resumes for $100,000+ Jobs	24.95	_____
_____ 101 Quick Tips for a Dynamite Resume	13.95	_____
_____ 201 Winning Cover Letters for the $100,000+ Jobs	24.95	_____
_____ 1500+ Key Words for 100,000+	14.95	_____
_____ Dynamite Cover Letters	14.95	_____
_____ Dynamite Resumes	14.95	_____
_____ Haldane's Best Cover Letters for Professionals	15.95	_____
_____ Haldane's Best Resumes for Professionals	15.95	_____
_____ High Impact Resumes and Letters	19.95	_____
_____ Sure-Hire Resumes	14.95	_____
_____ Winning Resumes	10.95	_____

INTERVIEWING: JOBSEEKERS

_____ 101 Dynamite Answers to Interview Questions	12.95	_____
_____ 101 Dynamite Questions to Ask at Your Job Interview	14.95	_____
_____ 101 Tough Interview Questions. . .	14.95	_____
_____ 111 Dynamite Ways to Ace Your Job Interview	13.95	_____
_____ Haldane's Best Answers to Tough Interview Questions	15.95	_____
_____ Interview for Success	15.95	_____
_____ Savvy Interviewing	10.95	_____

NETWORKING AND JOB SEARCHING TOOLS

_____ 100 Top Internet Job Sites	12.95	_____
_____ Dynamite Networking for Dynamite Jobs	15.95	_____

_____	Dynamite Tele-Search	12.95	_____
_____	Electronic Resumes	19.95	_____
_____	Employer's Guide to Recruiting on the Internet	24.95	_____
_____	Internet Resumes	14.95	_____

SALARY NEGOTIATIONS

_____	Dynamite Salary Negotiations	15.95	_____
_____	Get a Raise in 7 Days	14.95	_____
_____	Get More Money on Your Next Job	14.95	_____
_____	Negotiate Your Job Offer	14.95	

IMAGE AND ETIQUETTE

_____	Dressing Smart in the New Millennium	13.95	_____
_____	John Malloy's Dress for Success (For Men)	13.99	_____
_____	New Women's Dress for Success	12.99	_____
_____	Red Socks Don't Work	14.95	_____
_____	You've Only Got 3 Seconds	22.95	_____

INSPIRATION & EMPOWERMENT

_____	Beating Job Burnout	12.95	_____
_____	Big Things Happen When You Do the Little Things Right	15.00	_____
_____	Chicken Soup for the Soul Series	87.95	_____
_____	Do What You Love, the Money Will Follow	11.95	_____
_____	Get What You Deserve	23.00	_____
_____	If Life Is A Game, These Are the Rules	15.00	_____
_____	Seven Habits of Highly Effective People	14.00	

☞ **SUBTOTAL** $ _____

☞ Virginia residents add 4½% sales tax) _____

☞ Shipping/handling, Continental U.S., $5.00 + _____ $5.00
plus following percentages when **SUBTOTAL** is:

   ☐ $30-$100—multiply SUBTOTAL by 8% _____

   ☐ $100-$999—multiply SUBTOTAL by 7% _____

   ☐ $1,000-$4,999—multiply SUBTOTAL by 6% _____

   ☐ Over $5,000—multiply SUBTOTAL by 5% _____

☞   ☐ If shipped outside Continental US, add another 5% _____

☞ **TOTAL ENCLOSED** $_____

SHIP TO: (street address only for UPS or RPS delivery)

Name _____

Address _____

_____

_____

Telephone _____

I enclose ❑ Check ❑ Money Order in the amount of: $ _____

Charge $ _____ to ❑ Visa ❑ MC ❑ AmEx

Card # _____ Exp: _____ / _____

Signature _____

DISCOVER HUNDREDS OF ADDITIONAL RESOURCES ON THE WORLD WIDE WEB!

Looking for the newest and best books, directories, newsletters, wall charts, training programs, videos, computer software, and kits to help you land a job, negotiate a higher salary, or start your own business? Want to learn the most effective way to find a job in Asia or relocate to San Francisco? Are you curious about how to find a job 24 hours a day using the Internet or about what you'll be doing five years from now? Are you trying to keep up-to-date on the latest career resources, but are not able to find the latest catalogs, brochures, or newsletters on today's "best of the best" resources?

Welcome to the first virtual career bookstore on the Internet. Now you're only a click away with Impact Publications' electronic solution to the resource challenge. Visit this rich site to quickly discover everything you ever wanted to know about finding jobs, changing careers, and starting your own business—including many useful resources that are difficult to find in local bookstores and libraries. The site also includes what's new and hot, tips for job search success, and monthly specials. Check it out today!

www.impactpublications.com